Quarterly Essay

CONTENTS

Quarterly Essay is published four times a year by Black Inc., an imprint of Schwartz Publishing Pty Ltd
Publisher: Morry Schwartz

ISBN 1 86395 355 8

Subscriptions (4 issues): $49.95 a year within Australia incl. GST (Institutional subs. $59.95). Outside Australia $79.95. Payment may be made by Mastercard, Visa or Bankcard, or by cheque made out to Schwartz Publishing. Payment includes postage and handling.

To subscribe, fill out and post the subscription form on the last page of this essay, or subscribe online at:

www.quarterlyessay.com

Correspondence and subscriptions should be addressed to the Editor at:
Black Inc.
Level 5, 289 Flinders Lane
Melbourne VIC 3000 Australia
Phone: 61 3 9654 2000
Fax: 61 3 9654 2290
Email: quarterlyessay@blackincbooks.com
http://www.quarterlyessay.com

Editor: Peter Craven
Management: Sophy Williams
Managing Editor: Chris Feik
Editorial Co-ordinator: Caitlin Yates
Publicity: Meredith Kelly
Design: Guy Mirabella

Quarterly Essay aims to present significant contributions to political, intellectual and cultural debate. It is a magazine in extended pamphlet form and by publishing in each issue a single writer at a length of at least **20,000** words we hope to mediate between the limitations of the newspaper column, where there is the danger that evidence and argument can be swallowed up by the form, and the kind of full-length study of a subject where the only readership is a necessarily specialised one. *Quarterly Essay* aims for the attention of the committed general reader. Although it is a periodical which wants subscribers, each number of the journal is the length of a short book because we want our writers to have the opportunity to speak to the broadest possible audience without condescension or populist short-cuts. *Quarterly Essay* wants to get away from the tyranny that space limits impose in contemporary journalism and we give our essayists the space to express the evidence for their views and those who disagree with them the chance to reply at whatever length is necessary. *Quarterly Essay* will not be confined to politics but is centrally concerned with it. We are not interested in occupying any particular point on the political map and we hope to bring our readership the widest range of political and cultural opinion which is compatible with truth-telling, style and command of the essay form.

INTRODUCTION

Gideon Haigh's *Bad Company: The Cult of the CEO* is the tenth of the *Quarterly Essays* and something of a departure for us because it does not, in any obvious sense, emerge from a broad consensus of left-liberal opinion. On the contrary, Haigh is not only a devout believer in capitalism, he is someone who is not interested in the contemporary witch-hunt about the mad, bad CEOs who have destroyed their companies, crippled their shareholders and generally acted like criminals.

Or rather he is interested in this only as the symptom, *in extremis*, of a deeper disease. He cites John Kenneth Galbraith to the effect that there will always be an element of embezzlement in business and that different economic climates and different economic cycles will highlight it in different ways, nor is its perception wholly distinct from fashions and counter-fashions.

But the grosser examples of corporate misbehaviour, which inflame the Right and Left, are not Gideon Haigh's primary emphasis. What he is interested in is not the crooks *per se* but the wholly conventional captains of industry who we have elected to believe are the colossi of a market world of which they seem the emblems and the epitomes. What gets dubbed globalisation, Haigh remarks at one point, is simply the regnancy of the American way of managing economies of all kinds and what goes along with this is the apotheosis of the managers.

Not the managing directors, of course, that's yesterday's parlance — enshrining yesterday's modesties, it suggests that the wondermen are merely the first among equals. No, the CEO in his contemporary incarnation is possessed of the traditional *mana* of kinship and he (generally it's a he) is paid so royally that you have to wonder what blind faith is hedging him with such divinity.

Gideon Haigh takes the coldest possible view of all this. He simply does not believe that you can take an upper-level managerial axe-wielder (trained on exactly the same Harvard MBA doctrine as all the other axe-wielders) and turn him into a genius of business by fabricating a status for him as some kind of stakeholder (a term that irresistibly reminds Haigh of the world of *Dracula*).

Haigh believes that the system of paying the CEOs the earth represents the folly of believing that you can turn humdrum generals into Napoleons by the simple procedure of remunerating them as only a thaumaturge could sanely be rewarded. It is an attempt to create great entrepreneurs out of hireling managers by the flawed method of giving them equity and stock options.

It sounds like a good enough idea in theory – that the newly hired CEO will act more in the interests of his adoptive company if he has a stake in its fortunes – until you realise he can effortlessly divest himself of these interests to his own financial benefit when it happens to suit him.

There is also an inherent absurdity for Haigh in the idea of instantaneously rewarding the brilliant CEO when true wisdom in business is not likely to be measurable for years, sometimes many years, after the event.

We have become used to the spectacle of the new-style CEO who sacks some bewildering fraction of the staff (often people doing crucial jobs in companies with little fat) for the sake of the figures, as if this was an end in itself. We have also seen the kind of CEO – was Donald Rumsfeld, the Secretary for the War on Everything, in this category? – who window-dresses simply for the purpose of selling the shop.

Much of what passes as business doctrine these days is to Haigh just a fire lit by heretics. Hence his disdain for figures like "Chainsaw Al" Dunlap, who did not change the world of business to anyone's betterment apart from their own, they simply interpreted it as a graph for their egos and solaced themselves with dogs who could not talk back.

One of the distinctive things about Gideon Haigh's *Bad Company* is that it is written against the post-Iacocca CEOs from the conservative position of someone who has a deep belief in the history of sane business practice and sees it mocked by the mutations it has suffered, which are still slavishly valorised by the very people who scream about the crimes of the crooked CEOs without realising that much the greater problem is structural.

That's one reason why this *Quarterly Essay*, written in the wake of the HIH outrage and a general Australian wave of horror at CEOs gone crazy, is first of all a kind of history of business and is, secondly, so preoccupied with the American paradigm and the way it has impacted on international practice.

Haigh believes that you cannot offer a critique of contemporary business unless you are conscious of how much it comes out of the past and how radically it departs from it. He does not think you can understand the excesses of the Australian CEOs – even though his focus on them becomes closer as *Bad Company* moves towards its conclusions – unless you understand how parasitic they have been on an American model which is itself flawed but which has at times been efficacious in its own terms. (Haigh thinks that the celebrity-style American CEOs tend to be bad news but that at least they have increased profitability which is more than can be said for their marsupial brethren.)

Of course Haigh also has a fascination at once historical and satirical with both the enormities and the banalities of his subject. He can savour the creepiness of Henry Ford just as he can admire the far-seeing restraint of Alfred Sloan, the great head of General Motors, whose "impersonality" by contemporary standards of braggadocio and mercilessness is like T. S. Eliot compared to who ... Marilyn Manson?

That's not a Haigh comparison but metaphor and allusion abound in *Bad Company* which is an excavation of business history that manages to ally it with history proper and through history with literature. This is a meditation on the CEOs of a time of low morals that exhibits an attendant awareness of Dickens and Trollope not as adornments but as exemplifications of reality and which is spiced with the odd bit of de Tocqueville or Machiavelli because political hard talk has a perennial pertinence to the money game.

It is written in a style which combines the erudition of one of the nation's most accomplished business writers with the natural plumage and range of mind of a writer who is by inclination dandyish in vocabulary and locution and always willing to go down crooked byways that can sharpen our sense of sometimes dark matters.

Haigh is at every point a compelling writer even when he is dragging the reader through thickets of new information or – which will also happen, contrarily, with his business readers especially – when he is defying what is generally accepted as the wisdom of the world.

The world where the CEO is deemed to be a "genius" at least equal to a great actor or a great sportsman is a world in which that savant of the cricket oval Gideon Haigh refuses to believe. He never quite says that these CEOs are moral pygmies or cultural morons, but he has a very powerful sense of how banal they are and how crushingly mundane are the values they represent and the values that have brought about their election.

And for Gideon Haigh we are all responsible because it is the world view we have created as an alternative dogma beyond which we cannot see because its value rests and rests utterly on the void. These jumped-up job-cutters with their mean minds and their narrow skills, their human quality of admitting no humane culture except that of cliché. Forget the Adlers and the Williamses and all the particular configurations of greed and folly, the collective delusion that has created a race of exorbitant titans out of managers is one we have all subscribed to.

Cancellation is the only solution and Haigh's view of the subject is Ockhamite indeed. Who knows most about a company? The implication of this *Quarterly Essay* is quite plainly: the people who have devoted their lives to it, not the pig who comes in disguised as a silk purse because the position and the pay gleam like gold. Haigh is committed to the conservative tradition of business to such an extent that he will be mistaken for a radical ratbag. He even believes that some of the most qualified people to sit on boards could be drawn from the ranks (shock, horror) of retired middle management. Might they be stick-in-the-mud, disinclined to take risks, Haigh asks. Good on them.

Agnosticism of this order may sound like carol singing in no man's land and provoke fire from both sides. In any event this is a tough demythologising essay, scathing and elegant, which will be read with pleasure and discomfort by the widest range of readers.

It is an essay by a man who takes a delight in the history of business, its scurrilities and its high achievements, who has never mistaken the sound of money for the music of the spheres.

Peter Craven

BAD COMPANY | The Cult of the CEO

Gideon Haigh

Ray Williams, it is said, prided himself on his manly bearing, favouring smart, dark suits tailored to his tautened physique, and always greeting visitors with a firm, sincere, double-handed handshake. He preferred, too, to keep the wider world at a distance, buying the house of his Mosman neighbour for $5 million to preserve his privacy, and commissioning a private chapel for his walled Lake Macquarie retreat rather than expose his family to the prying eyes of a public congregation. That poise did not desert him last year when he became Australia's best-known and most-maligned chief executive officer, at the royal commission investigating the collapse of the HIH insurance group which he had headed for thirty years. He seemed cool, detached, crisply laundered, oblivious to the media's *enfilade* of enquiries, his thin, unparting lips shaped in a mirthless smile. His severe countenance belied the excess involved in HIH's $5.3 billion failure in March 2001.

Justice Neville Owen's report, released on 16 April 2003, begins with a Shakespearean flourish: "Beware the Ides of March." History's

most famous unheeded warning, says Owen, "resonated eerily" throughout the commission, HIH's "shambling journey towards oblivion" having
begun long before. The reader braces instinctively for a story of cabal
and conspiracy, of hubris and nemesis – and the judge comes to bury
the CEO not to praise him, citing "blind faith in a leadership that was ill-
equipped for the task", in which "the hand and influence of Williams
were paramount". HIH, it emerges, spent tomorrow's money today in
order to satisfy its cravings for premium income, plunging headlong into
the acquisitions of CIC in June 1995 and FAI in September 1998 as it
also threw good money after bad in the United States and United
Kingdom. And on these condemnations did the attention of journalists
naturally alight, translating into damning headlines: "Blind faith, naked
greed", "HIH boss blamed for collapse", "HIH chief faces jail" and, of
course, in anticipation of the salutary smack of firm government, "Costello
pledges justice for all".

Yet what detains the eye in Owen's report is what might be considered
a corporate variation on Hannah Arendt's "banality of evil": the mun-
danity of mismanagement. HIH, says the judge, was "not a case where
wholesale fraud or embezzlement abounded", and "by and large the people who were involved were not inherently bad or in some way set upon
being part of a corporate disaster." After three decades in charge, Williams
was unrivalled in "authority" and "influence". But his control depended
on there being "insufficient ability and independence of mind in … the
organisation to see what had to be done and what had to be stopped or
avoided"; failure was as much an outcome of "a culture of apparent indif-
ference or deliberate disregard on the part of those responsible for the
well-being of the company". Justice Owen reveals an organisation that
was "often flying blind". Its electronic financial system provided incorri-
gibly incomplete and inaccurate information. Its general ledger had
unreconciled accounts dating back to 1995. The reporting regime was
lax, the audit committee misconstituted, the budgeting process misconceived, the preparation of financial information was being manipulated

by lower-level managers; the judge worries explicitly that preoccupation with bosses and boards "may cause to be overlooked the reality of the necessarily greater part that executives and other employees play in the day-to-day running of many corporate businesses". And all this occurred in an environment which was, from the mid-1990s, one of falling interest rates, lower investment returns, poorer premium rates, costlier underwriting losses and escalating claims.

By far the shrewdest reading of the report came from Trevor Sykes, our foremost connoisseur of corporate collapse, in the *Australian Financial Review*: "HIH was run so badly it is surprising it lasted as long as it did. If there were any fundamental mistake they did not make, it must have been an oversight." Even with a vainglorious boss wielding unilateral power, a management heedless of the morrow, a riven board, avaricious associates, compromised advisers and a succession of destructive deals in hazardous commercial conditions, HIH took a long time to die; indeed, for much of its lifetime as a listed company, its share price was rising. This is not the stuff of headlines, but it is the stuff of this essay. Business failure is complex – and so is business success. If it sounds like a form of exculpation to imply that CEOs aren't as bad as we are inclined to imagine them, then it also follows that they were not, are not and never will be as good as they and others pretend.

That CEOs have become our new hate figures is partly because our disillusionment stems from a prior faith. As little as three years ago, when we were still toasting the *belle époque* in equities, many figures who are now reviled were revered. And if we are not in thrall to business, we are certainly complicit in a model of the world it finds amenable. Business rhetoric pervades the language of our politicians, our professionals, our academics, even our athletes. Business customs have infiltrated schools, universities, the public service, even volunteer organisations. Business schools churn out newly minted MBAs. Bookshops devote whole walls to books with titles like *How To Become CEO*, *How To Act Like a CEO*, and *CEO Logic: How To Think and Act Like a Chief Executive*. Business leadership, publishers would have us believe, is a timeless art, practised since antiquity, even when its exponents — such as Jesus Christ, Sun Tzu, Alexander the Great, Sir Ernest Shackleton, General George Patton, Thomas Jefferson and Elizabeth I — were unconscious of their acumen.

It's now almost a commonplace to assert that the well-being of a nation hinges on its corporations' competitiveness, and thus on the vision and vitality of those running them. When Lou Gerstner was invited to restore the fortunes of IBM a decade ago, he was invited to regard it as his patriotic duty. "You owe it to America to take the job," he was told by James Burke, Johnson & Johnson's *éminence grise*. When WorldCom's market value peaked at $us120 billion in June 1999, President Bill Clinton accepted an invitation to its Mississippi headquarters from founder Bernie Ebbers. "I came here today because you are the symbol of 21st-century America," Clinton eulogised. "You are the embodiment of what I want for the future." Exposed within a couple of years later to have overstated its profits by $us9 billion, WorldCom proved to embody something else entirely.

Corporate leadership as preparation for high office is also an idea whose time has come. Businessmen turned politicians are increasingly widespread: some succeed, like Silvio Berlusconi of Italy's Fininvest; some are thwarted, like Hyundai founder Chung Ju Yung in South Korea. Some even blossom into statesmen: Kofi Annan, the secretary general of the United Nations, has a masters in management from MIT, and once ran the Ghana Tourist Development Company.

In the United States — where the phrase "chief executive" originated about 150 years ago to denote the president himself — the nexus is especially strong. Vice-president Dick Cheney (energy services group Halliburton), commerce secretary Don Evans (energy services group Tom Brown Inc.), labour secretary Elaine Chao (United Way of America), White House chief-of-staff Andrew Card Jr (American Automobile Manufacturers Association), treasury secretary John Snow (CSX) and defence secretary Donald Rumsfeld (General Instruments and pharmaceutical group G. D.

Searle) are all former CEOs. Rumsfeld featured in *Fortune* magazine's inaugural intake of "America's Ten Toughest Bosses" in April 1 9 8 0; *The Rumsfeld Way* (2 0 0 2) suggests that he persecutes corporate bureaucracies as vehemently as any "axis of evil". Though at the height of Gulf War II there were many dark mutterings about the malign influence of religion in the White House, the Bush administration is more of a CEOcracy than a theocracy, headed as it is not only by the first president to hold a Harvard MBA, but the first to have been investigated by the Securities and Exchange Commission. Whatever the US's hegemonic pretensions in the Middle East, its leaders are restrained by fiscal rectitude: these days, even war has to come in on time and on budget.

In a society where we look one another right in the wallet, CEOs certainly stand tall: seldom in history have we elected to reward a caste so richly. When Graef Crystal published a wide-ranging critique of executive rewards in 1991, describing a twenty-year period in which American CEOs had hiked their own pay 4 0 0 per cent, he called it *In Search of Excess*. No one had to look far: CEO compensation in the US surged another 5 3 5 per cent in the 1 9 9 0s. In part, this was a natural outcome of the increasing use of equity, in the form of stock options, as a component of remuneration. But only in part — the increase actually outstripped all conceivable correlatives. The value of the top 5 0 0 stocks increased about 3 0 0 per cent over the same period, profits about doubled, and average weekly wages grew only a third. In 1 9 9 1, the standard big-company CEO in the US earned 1 4 0 times the pay of the average worker; the multiple is now nearer 5 0 0 times. CEO pay comes in many varieties, with a common shade of gold: golden hellos, golden handcuffs, golden handshakes and, should it come to that, golden parachutes, a severance package payable in the event of a change of control.

The recipients, at least, have encountered no difficulty in rationalising their rewards. A poll of *Fortune* 1000 CEOs last year revealed that 8 7 per cent thought their pay was just what they deserved, 1 1 per cent thought they were still underpaid, and only 2 per cent confessed to feeling over-rewarded. Others are uneasy. "The past decade has witnessed the greatest transfer of wealth from shareholders to workers in the history of the US economy," remarked *New Yorker's* James Surowiecki last year. "Unfortunately, the workers were almost all ensconced in the executive suite." Some are downright hostile. In her new corporate *j'accuse, Pigs at the Trough*, Arianna Huffington envisions a suburb, CEOville, whose residents have subtly revised the Declaration of Independence to read: "All men are endowed by their creator with certain inalienable rights, that among these are stock options, golden parachutes, and the reckless pursuit of limitless wealth." Though the figures aren't so gross in Australia, nor the attitudes so brazen, they remain impressive. CEOs at our top 1 0 0 companies enjoyed salaries averaging $ 2 million in the last financial year – a 3 8 per cent annual increase. They now earn in a week roughly what the average worker collects in a year, even before their equity rewards are factored in. At least one CEO, Paul Anderson of BHP Billiton, was moved to remark that executive remuneration was "totally out of control" – just, mind you, as he was about to pocket $ 1 9 million for services rendered.

With higher pay, of course, have come greater expectations. "They [CEOs] have become personalities in a drama," observed Michel Albert in his perceptive *Capitalisme contre Capitalisme*, "and they must live up to the script or disappoint an audience of millions." Investors no longer keep disappointment to themselves either. In a survey of 2 5 0 0 companies last year, consultants Booz Allen found that turnover of CEOs had increased 5 3 per cent between 1 9 9 5 and 2 0 0 1, while the number leaving office because of failure to meet performance criteria had grown 1 3 0 per cent. According to the corporate relations group Burson-Marsteller, CEOs entrusted with turnarounds will in most instances have only one chance to make a mark: the market allows about eight months to develop a strategy, nineteen months to bolster the share price, twenty-one months to improve earnings. If nothing has changed, or not enough, the process is repeated. The phenomenon, christened "CEO churning", has some powerful proponents. Warren Buffett, the most sagacious investor of his generation, led the putsch ousting Doug Ivester in December 1999 after eighteen wretched months at Coca-Cola; and it was William Clay Ford Jnr, no less, who in October 2001 seized the controls at the corporation founded by his great-grandfather when its boss of less than three years, Jac Nasser, threatened to run it off the road.

At one time, Europeans would have deplored the wastage inherent in *le capitalisme sauvage du modèle anglo-saxon*. Yet attrition in their CEO ranks has recently been almost as great. In France, entertainment mogul *manqué* Jean-Marie Messier was sacked from Vivendi Universal for his thriftless ways. In Germany, Thomas Middelhoff lost his job at Europe's biggest media company, Bertelsmann, after estranging its powerful Mohn family. France Telecom, Deutsche Telecom and Telecom Italia all churned bosses within eighteen months. Corporate comeuppance has even become a feature of Asian business with the indictments for accounting fraud in South Korea of senior executives at Posco, the world's second-biggest steelmaker, and SK Group, the country's third-largest *chaebol*. In Australia, meanwhile, ritual executive sacrifice has caught on with a vengeance: the average CEO now lasts about four years. A quarter of our top 100 companies have turned over their bosses in the last two years. Retailer Gerry Harvey has likened the Business Council of Australia to Alzheimer's Disease: you're always making new friends. Some departures have been spectacular: Colin Chandler fell fastest, leaving Open Telecommunication after six months; Paul Batchelor fell farthest, being defenestrated from AMP last September.

Yet this phenomenon concerns more than lavish tributes to success and severe penalties for failure. A disturbing perversity of the market over the last few years has been the ease, not to say the alacrity, with which failure has been rewarded, and the way deceit and dishonesty have not only been condoned but craved — a process involving the collusion of docile auditors, credulous analysts and supine shareholders, and exposed, as often happens, only by the interruption of a long-running bull cycle. An axiom of the securities market is that "a rising tide lifts all boats".

WorldCom, Adelphia, Qwest, Global Crossing, Sunbeam, ImClone and others have demonstrated the truth of Warren Buffett's corollary that receding waters reveal who's been swimming naked.

No corporate humbling has been quite so complete as that at Enron – the Houston energy dynamo that *Fortune* rated "America's most innovative corporation" for six consecutive years. Its deepest well of innovation turned out to be the one from which chairman Ken Lay, CEO Jeffrey Skilling and chief financial officer Andrew Fastow drew their accounts. Enron's balance sheet resembled one of those eerily perfected Hollywood bodies: assets toned, chiselled and always shot from the right angles; liabilities tastefully liposuctioned away. And Lay, Skilling, Fastow and their confederates charged a hefty price for this seductive illusion. In 2001, Enron dispersed $us680 million among its executive cadre: Lay alone pocketed $us67.4 million in salary, bonuses and stock options. These sums did not seem so vast in an organisation the seventh-largest in the US, with revenues of $us100 billion. But in November 2001, the effects of its concealment and profiteering finally took their toll. When a restatement of earnings resulted in a credit rating downgrade and the reconsolidation of off-balance structures increased debt by $3.9 billion, Enron's credibility and counterparty status crumbled. Four thousand employees lost their jobs; within months, 85,000 at Enron's accomplice, accounting firm Arthur Andersen, had lost theirs as well.

Of all the individual idols toppled in this recent executive *Götterdämmerung*, meanwhile, none was grander or more graven than the corporate turnaround specialist "Chainsaw Al" Dunlap. He did not just seek profit at all costs – he preached it, sometimes irascibly, always impatiently, styling himself as an implacable enemy of paternalism, sentimentality and discretionary spending. Although Dunlap purported to tone flaccid corporate muscle, his traditional approach was to impose a crash diet based on sweeping austerities and redundancies. His chief triumph was an eighteen-month tenure at Scott Paper: the company's stock price grew 225 per cent as it shed assets worth $us2.4 billion and 11,000 workers preparatory to acquisition by Kimberly-Clark in December 1995. "Did I earn that?" Dunlap asked of his $us100 million in equity spoils, earned at $us165,000 a day. "Damn right I did. I'm a superstar in my field, much like Michael Jordan in basketball and Bruce Springsteen in rock'n'roll." He even presumed to improve on Harry Truman's dictum that if you wanted a friend, you should get a dog. "I'm not taking any chances," said Dunlap. "I've got two dogs." On the cover of Dunlap's 1996 autobiography, Mean Business, Stetson University law professor Charles Elson stated that Chainsaw Al had "sparked a revolution on the American corporate scene ... by demonstrating that you can entrepreneurialise the large-scale public corporation".

When Dunlap was called on to "entrepreneurialise" the appliance giant Sunbeam in June 1996, his formula proved as robust as ever – at first, anyway. Huge write-offs rinsed its balance sheet; huge lay-offs wrung $us225 million from costs; the share price quadrupled. This time, however, no bidders appeared. Dunlap fell back on the old-fashioned accounting trick of loading wholesalers' shelves with product and booking the proceeds as revenue. The products did not sell, returns sent Sunbeam reeling, "increasingly desperate measures" to disguise the impact failed, and directors rebelled. Their leader: Charles Elson, seized by the zeal of the apostate.

The response to iniquity has been the usual mix of regulation and retribution. The US Congress rushed the Sarbanes-Oxley Act into law last July, requiring that CEOs and CFOs swear in front of a notary that their latest annual and quarterly filings contain no "untrue statement" and omit no "material fact". The Australian Stock Exchange's rules on corporate governance announced in April have set a premium on independent directors and further disclosure. And at present, there's less interest in the kind of stocks we buy than in the kind used in conjunction with rotten fruit. In a new series on "family-friendly" Pax TV, Just Cause, an avenging paralegal is entrusted with "cleaning up America ... one crooked CEO at a time" – at that rate, it could run and run.

But if there's something amiss with our models of corporate governance, then we are all deeply implicated. We have placed our trust in commercial pragmatism – and a very particular form of it, for to speak of CEOs at all is to enfold an American idea of corporate command. As the Canadian organisational theorist Henry Mintzberg noted drily, what we call globalisation is more often simply "American management spreading round the world". To understand our own discontents, then, it is on the evolution of this form of management that we must concentrate.

RICH WHITE MEN

Who are CEOs and where do they come from? At the simplest level, big businesses are still run overwhelmingly by men. Women who've bubbled to the surface have tended to attract more attention than their companies – to their advantage in good times, to their detriment in bad. The *Economist* outlines the vicious circle: "There are not enough female executives, which means that those who do emerge, get over-hyped, which increases the chance of failure (real or perceived), which makes companies more nervous about appointing female chief executives." This partly explains why female CEOs have seldom differentiated themselves significantly from the male of the species, even in terms of susceptibility to the temptations of corporate excess: witness the $us50 million that Jill Barad collected after presiding over a disastrous acquisition at toy giant Mattel, and the $us44 million "golden parachute" that made Linda Wachner unsackable at fading fashion group Warnaco.

It could be said that women shape corporations in other ways. For instance, the three most admired American bosses of the last twenty years – Wal-Mart's Sam Walton, IBM's Lou Gerstner and General Electric's Jack Welch – were raised in matriduxies. Walton's mother was "a pretty special motivator" who was "extremely ambitious for her kids"; Gerstner's "drove us toward excellence, accomplishment and success" by being "enormously disciplined, hard-working, and ambitious for all her children"; Welch's fortified him with "blunt, unyielding admonitions that ring in my head every day", and habits for which he later became renowned: "She checked constantly to see if I did my homework, in much the same way that I continually follow up work today." They also came from religious households: Walton was a Methodist, Welch and Gerstner strict Catholics. American religion is withal a coat of many colours. WorldCom's Bernie Ebbers and Enron's Ken Lay were both bible-bashing Baptists: Ebbers began board and stockholder meetings with a prayer; Lay, a preacher's son, solemnly declared during the

Californian power crisis three years ago, "I believe in God and I believe in free markets."

Such surveys are *au fond* largely futile. The backgrounds of successful business leaders present few obvious patterns. Most guides to the brains behind corporations reveal little beyond their conventionality. In *Entering Tiger Country*, their survey of "how ideas are shaped in an organisation", Jean Lammiman and Michel Syrett turned up some strikingly unenlightening information: a sixth of CEOs surveyed had found business inspiration through a fictional character, a fifth through a historical personage like Winston Churchill, while more than half had had their best ideas while in relaxed settings like travelling, walking the dog or listening to music. In *The Mind of the CEO*, Jeffrey Garten sought to demonstrate that "top business leaders are the people who best understand the effects of change, technology, globalisation", yet found them even duller on the subject than most politicians. It's not even as though CEOs are distinguished by superior intelligence – a puzzle that perplexed the first American executive paid more than $us1 million, Charles Schwab, US Steel's inaugural president, a century ago: "Here I am, a not over-good business man, a second-rate engineer. I can make poor mechanical drawings. I play the piano after a fashion. In fact, I am one of those proverbial jack-of-all-trades who are usually failures. Why I am not, I can't tell you." Schwab was also an early victim of the preference boards evince for CEOs with inconspicuous private lives. With a Mr Toad-like taste for speed and spending, he fell out with J. P. Morgan after two well-publicised roulette wins at Monte Carlo in January 1902. An image of domestic serenity remains advisable. When Michael Eisner was seeking the top job at Disney, he gained crucial support from big investor Sid Bass when a family photo in a wholesome magazine profile "reassured him that I didn't fit the stereotype of a wild, partying Hollywood executive".

It is by what they do, rather than who they are, that CEOs differentiate themselves. Mark Twain once observed that if work were so great, "the rich would have hogged it long ago". If he studied the Stakhanovite executives of today, he might decide that they have. Three-quarters of American CEOs work more than sixty hours a week, re-designing hearth and home around the contours of duty. They start early. Hewlett-Packard's Carly Fiorina rises at 4.30 a.m. and jogs on a treadmill while checking her e-mails. They finish late. DaimlerChrysler's Jürgen Schrempp believes in disarming managers with alcohol: "You never hear the truth from your subordinates until after ten in the evening." Of course, hard work and long work are not the same as good work: Ray Williams typically logged fifteen hours a day at the office.

As far as recreation is concerned, the traditional diversion has been golf, usually with business talked as fairways are traversed. "I've met some of the world's greatest human beings playing golf," opines Jack Welch, revealing that part of the selection process for his successor at General Electric was a golf day with directors – suitable candidates, by definition, played a decent game. But times are changing. Profiling a new generation of bosses last November, *Fortune* said, "Shockingly, most of them don't even engage in that classic CEO pastime: golf." There's no opportunity. The CEO spends a goodly proportion of time simply in transit, a fashion both risky and irksome. Chris Jones of advertising giant J. Walter Thompson resigned in January 2001 after suffering deep vein thrombosis on a flight from New York to Geneva. A dig made by BHP Billiton directors when they ousted Brian Gilbertson in January 2003 was that he was "always on a plane".

The CEO's relationship to money, meanwhile, is complex. Practically, money means little to them. They have more than they will ever need, and in the course of an average day will spend little of their own: the company charge card caters for quotidian needs; a cheap corporate loan covers anything more elaborate. Yet financial security seems to breed personal insecurity: "How much am I earning?" "How much is he earning?" "Why aren't I earning as much as him?" Drug giant Novartis's CEO Daniel Vasella confessed last year to have gone through a stage of blinding obsession with his rewards: "The strange part is, the more I made, the more

I got preoccupied with money. When suddenly I didn't have to think about money as much, I found myself thinking increasingly about it." So much for the theory of money's instrumentality, that it is useful only for what it can buy. In the executive suite, money confers status; it becomes an abstract indicator of being.

Those who believe regulation and transparency can solve all social ills should acknowledge that their consequence in this instance has been perfectly perverse. More information about CEO salaries was meant to curb excess; *au contraire*, excess has exceeded itself. The phrase "internationally competitive" has taken on conspicuously opposite meanings where top and bottom of the salary scale are concerned: while workers are enjoined to price their labour to compete with the cheapest rival, CEOs seek convergence with the highest common denominator. Consider the impact of trans-Atlantic mergers. American bosses, of course, are paid far more than their European counterparts; an American executive who was asked why he wanted so much money once replied simply, "It's the score." But Europeans increasingly agree. Finding himself surrounded by better-paid American peers a year ago, GlaxoSmithKline CEO Jean-Pierre Garnier demanded a five-fold pay increase to $us31 million. Garnier encountered what economists call an "outrage constraint" – he was stymied at the last by restive investors. But GSK's advertised commitment to "aligning its incentive plans with those of its pharmaceutical peer group" should ensure that no sense of inferiority lingers.

Money, of course, *does* buy things, and *in extremis* their acquisition can become compulsive. Tyco International's disgraced boss Dennis Kozlowski became notorious for his $us6000 shower curtain, $us15,000 dog-shaped umbrella stand, $us2900 gilded wastebasket and $us2.1 million birthday party for his wife in Sardinia (where an ice sculpture of Michelangelo's David dispensed Stoli through its appendage). Hearings at the HIH Royal Commission disclosed that a comparable squandermania affected Ray Williams, who bestowed Cuban cigars worth $1600 on a favourite debtor, dispensed $7000 Baume and Mercier gold watches to staff, and in one fortnight spent as much as $9 0 0 0 at a veritable *Michelin Guide* of restaurants. These items, though, were merely about being rich: for Kozlowski and Williams, the *coup* lay in leading their baroque lifestyles at company expense. The CEO is not simply another "conspicuous consumer", but a "conspicuous earner". And the earnings come not simply from contracted emoluments, bonuses, stock and golden gimmies, but in the appurtenances of office: the top-floor office eyrie, the limousine, the personal assistant, the entertainment budget and that modern equivalent of Cleopatra's barge, the executive jet. In its reliance on perquisites, the management of the modern corporation is reminiscent of the *ancien régime,* in which de Tocqueville found each group "differentiated from the rest by its right to petty privileges, even the least of which was regarded as a token of its exalted status". And by the time you are a CEO, the privileges are far from petty. Even the corporate HQ can be thought of as a form of gratification, of ego if not of income. No wonder so many bosses down the years have invested so extravagantly in head offices. And no wonder it has often foredoomed them, like the Sears Roebuck Tower, which as a monument to its boss's *folie de grandeur* attracted the epithet "Gordon Metcalf's Last Erection", and Coles Myer's forbidding "Battlestar Galactica" at Tooronga, which CEO Brian Quinn swapped for a smaller enclosure at Her Majesty's pleasure.

How should we picture the CEO at work? If we carry an image at all, it may be something like a field-marshal hovering over an ordinance map in his chateau, pushing tin soldiers here and toy cannons there, then barking orders at his staff officers. And while most management thinkers would now dismiss this picture as archaic, it contains a kernel of truth. Ideas of hierarchy and strategy in corporations are direct transpositions from the military. When management education began, in fact, where was one to look but the armed forces? Joseph Wharton told students in 1 8 9 0 that the business school named in his honour would "instil a sense of the coming strife" in which each manager would be "a soldier". As John Kay has also noted, the connection is, well ... kinda cool: "What boy (and most chief executives are men) has not dreamt of destroying his opponents with his new technology or his ingenuity? What youth has not identified with the great field generals of history ... inspiring their men to heroic feats with a few well-chosen words of encouragement and inspiration?" Thus the free indulgence in military metaphor by CEOs from Lee Iacocca ("I was the general in the war to save Chrysler") to Larry Ellison ("My ideal vice-president would be Genghis Khan"), not to mention *delenda est Carthago* mission statements like Nike's "Crush Adidas", Kohmatsu's "Encircle Caterpillar", Kao's "KPG" ("Kill Procter & Gamble") and Honda's "Yamaha Wo Tsubusu!" ("We will crush, squash, slaughter Yamaha!").

This metaphor, however, has its limits. Business isn't a zero-sum game. Success derives from your creation, not others' destruction. Nor should business, Kay observes, ever encourage valour:

> Military history abounds with stories of heroism in the face of adversity — Horatio defending the bridge, Custer's last stand, the charge of the Light Brigade ... But if General Custer or Lord Raglan had been businessmen, we should not have wished to have been their employees or to have bought their shares, and I would not myself have wished to invest in Horatio either. Fighting against overwhelming odds may sometimes be necessary military strategy. It is almost never a sensible business strategy.

The reality of executive life is more prosaic. Still perhaps the best guide is Henry Mintzberg's 1973 study, *The Nature of Managerial Work*. Having spent time with five CEOs in different industries and surveyed the contents of a sizeable sample of management diaries, Mintzberg concluded that the traditional roles of planning, organisation, co-ordination and control had little bearing on executive routines. Only 10 per cent of their activities took more than an hour:

> The CEOs met a steady stream of callers and mail from the moment they arrived in the morning until they left in the evening ... The traditional literature notwithstanding, the job of managing does not breed reflective planners; the manager responds to stimuli as

an individual who is conditioned by his job to prefer live to delayed action.

The fragmentation of the executive's time was strangely intrinsic to his stimulation:

> Jumping from topic to topic, he thrives on interruptions and, more often than not, disposes of items in ten minutes or less. Though he may have fifty projects going, all are delegated. He juggles them, checking each one periodically before sending it back into orbit.

His subjects, Mintzberg decided, were:

> fundamentally indistinguishable from their counterparts of 1 0 0 years ago (or 1 0 0 0 years ago, for that matter). The information they need differs, but they seek it in the same way; by word of mouth. Their decisions concern modern technology, but the procedures they use are still the same as the procedures of the nineteenth century.

Much, of course, has changed in thirty years, though one's impressions are generally that more has meant worse. Mintzberg has since likened management to sex, in that "you are supposed to figure it out but nobody tells you what to do." And this, it should be said, suits some. Jack Welch relished his job's disorder:

> Being a CEO is the nuts! A whole jumble of thoughts come to mind: Over the Top. Wild. Fun. Outrageous. Crazy. Passions. Perpetual motion. The give-and-take. Meetings into the night. Incredible friendships. Fine wine. Celebrations. Great golf courses. Big decisions in the real game. Crises and pressure. Lots of swings. A few home runs. The thrill of winning. The pain of losing. It's as good as it gets!

Up to a point, Lord Welch. If you're turning over a subject every ten minutes, how effective can you be? Even improved information technology is a mixed blessing for the modern CEO. He knows more, in terms of real-time intelligence from market frontiers – what's selling, what's not, who's gaining, who's slipping behind. But he also knows less – such specialist knowledge as he had begins at once to slip out of date, and his dependence on the expertise of others grows. Frankly, the company makes profits in ways he barely understands. In recent Australian history, Pasminco's $800 million misadventure in currency hedging and National Australia Bank's $4 billion risk-management bungle with American mortgage processor HomeSide come readily to mind.

So these developments are both new and not: the CEO's has always been an awkward role, of power and helplessness, of presence and absence. He makes decisions, but delegates most of their implementation. He knows things, but mostly what others, with superior knowledge of their respective areas, tell him. One of the most considered summaries is "The Dilemma of Corporation Man" by J. Irwin Miller, forty years the chief of Cummins Engine of Columbus, Indiana. A Rhodes scholar who studied philosophy and played the violin, Miller became so famous for his philanthropy and liberalism that he made it onto Richard Nixon's "enemies list". But as he explained in *Fortune* in August 1959, his job filled him with humility, and sometimes despair:

> To illustrate, let us suppose we can see inside the head of the president of a large manufacturing organisation. His company employs 20,000 people and operates half a dozen plants. It distributes its products in every state and in many foreign countries, and – most frightening of all – it has competitors. Now let us suppose that these competitors are extremely vigorous, and that our president knows that to maintain his share of the market and to make earnings which will please his directors, he must accomplish the following very quickly: design and perfect a brand-new and more advanced line of products; tool up these products in such a way as to permit higher quality and lower costs than his competitors; purchase new machinery; arrange major additional long-term financing. At the same time, his corporation's labor contract is up for negotiation, and this must be re-written in such a way as to obtain good employee response and yet make no more concessions than do his competitors. Sales coverage of all customers has to be intensified, and sales costs reduced. Every one of these objectives must be accomplished simultaneously, and ahead of similar efforts on the part of his competitors

– or the future of the company is in great danger. Every head of a corporation lives every day with the awareness that it is quite possible to go broke. At the same time he lives with the awareness that he cannot possibly accomplish a single one of these objectives. The actual work will have to be accomplished by numerous individuals, some actually unknown to him, most of them many layers removed from his direct influence in the organisation. It is because of this the president becomes frantic … He becomes dogmatic. He issues orders. He says things are jolly well going to be done this way and no other. He says the company's negotiators are not to give in on the union's demands for premium pay or the union shop. He says every salesman must make so many calls each day. He says you can't add a single person to this office, which has already got too many people in it. And he pounds the table every time he says these things. For he feels that this great, vast and ponderous organisation is his enemy and that inside its faceless exterior all his plans, his programs, his timetables will be diluted, slowed down, and ultimately defeated. Success seems to him to have come only in rare instances, and to have been of a temporary and ephemeral nature. He thinks of himself as being in a race that has no finish line. And his real antagonist is neither the customer, nor his bankers, nor the union. His real antagonist is the organisation.

The current debate about the role and renown of CEOs, then, seems one-dimensional – in its fixation with the CEO's control of corporations, it overlooks the degree to which the corporation controls its CEO. It will be the argument of this essay that paying outsized sums to CEOs is not simply socially offensive but intellectually difficult to justify – for reasons, moreover, inseparable from the development and character of the corporation itself.

The modern industrial corporation is the slow-ripened fruit of centuries, with origins stretching back to the Renaissance. It springs chiefly from three developments – the financial innovation of double-entry book-keeping, which allowed a separation between individuals and their commercial activities; the structural concept of the joint-stock company, pooling the resources of a group of investors and answerable to a board of directors; and the legal idea of limited liability. Of these, the third is perhaps most important to our story. Before limited liability, a person who had invested either individually or in partnership risked their whole worth: debtors' prisons were full of inadvertent and honourable failures. Few outside the founders and their kin would buy shares unless they either knew the firm's principals personally or could otherwise monitor its doings. Under limited liability – first permitted on restricted bases in the early nineteenth century, and finally made available to all companies by the legislature of New Jersey in 1846 – stockholders could not be held liable for the corporation's misdeeds.

At the dawn of capitalism, firms had been run by founders and, if they lasted that long, their heirs. By relieving shareholders of the need for unwavering vigilance, limited liability explicitly foresaw firms outliving their first generation under the guidance of a new class: the salaried manager.

This, it was swiftly recognised, entailed tensions. Much like modern parents anguishing about the theory and practice of child care, owners experienced pangs about entrusting their enterprises to hirelings. Charles Dickens dramatised their unease in *Dombey and Son* (1848). For all the Bounderbys, Gradgrinds and Merdles who came later, Dickens created no business relationship quite so intriguing as that between capitalist Paul Dombey, who thinks he is in charge of his firm of merchants, and manager James Carker, who knows he is. When the novel opens, Dombey is at his pinnacle:

> The earth was made for Dombey and Son to trade in and the sun and moon were made to give them light. Rivers and seas were formed to float their ships; rainbows gave them promise of fair weather; winds blew for or against their enterprises' stars and planets circled in their orbits, to preserve inviolate a system of which they were the centre.

When this "colossus of commerce" speaks, the world listens. His most famous speech, to his son, extols the virtues of wealth: "Money, Paul, can do anything ..."

Yet it has not acquired him the loyalty of Carker, "sly of manner, sharp of tooth, soft of foot, watchful of eye, oily of tongue, cruel of heart, nice of habit". When Dombey is distracted by his son's death, Carker uses his absences to "explore the mysteries of books and papers, with the patient progress of a man who was dissecting the minutest nerves and fibres of his subject", constructing "a labyrinth of which only he held the clue". Having sedulously scuttled the business, Carker then takes off with Dombey's second wife, though not before pouring out to his brother a timeless lament of the embittered manager:

> There is not a man employed here, standing between myself and the lowest in place ... who wouldn't be glad at heart to see his master humbled: who does not hate him, secretly: who does not wish him evil rather than good: and who would not turn upon him, if he had the power and boldness. The nearer to his favour, the nearer to his insolence, the closer to him, the farther from him. That's the creed here! ... Bah! There's not one among them, but if he had at once the power, and the wit and daring to use it, would not scatter Dombey's pride and lay it low, as ruthlessly as I rake out these ashes.

Dombey and Son was a strikingly subtle conception of where business had been and was headed with ownership and control decisively separated. In Carker's death beneath a locomotive's wheels, there is even a certain symbolic piquancy; it would be in American railyards, junctions, stations and sidings that the manager first took advantage of his empowerment. While the "Gilded Age", stretching roughly from the end of the Civil War to the turn of the century, is popularly associated with the kleptocracy of

Vanderbilts, Goulds and Fisks, railways also demanded more managers: managers more dispersed and more autonomous, observing controls, policies, corporate structures and reporting lines.

As often occurs, it required a crisis for an awareness of need to dawn. In his "Report on Avoiding Collisions and Governing the Employees" following a collision in October 1841, investigating engineer George Whistler saw the solution in "drawing solid lines of authority and communication for the railroad's administration, maintenance and operation". The line was divided into three contiguous operating divisions, each with an assistant master of transportation reporting to the board, roadmaster, senior mechanic and foreman. These ideas caught on. Erie Railroad's general superintendent Daniel McCallum had a particularly elaborate vision, harnessing the new-fangled telegraph to collect hourly reports from superintendents of geographic sections, and daily bulletins from conductors, agents and engineers. *American Railroad Journal* found his pioneering organisational diagram so mind-boggling that it offered lithographed copies for $ 1.

But the ablest manager – and really the first CEO as we would understand it – was J. Edgar Thomson. Pennsylvania Railroad, of which he was president and chairman, was the first big organisation run by management on behalf of a mostly passive group of investors. An engineer who had begun his career as a rodman in a survey crew, Thomson presided over an expansion of Pennsylvania's network from 250 miles to 6000 miles, and a diversification into mining its own coal, making its own steel and running its own steamships between London and Philadelphia. Most importantly, he honeycombed the Pennsylvania with managers, including a head office with discrete operating, accounting, treasury and legal departments. At its zenith in the early 1890s the Pennsylvania employed 110,000 people – America's army and navy ran to fewer than 40,000. "We are specialists," gushed a colleague, "that is, pygmies. Thomson was great in everything – operating, traffic, motive power, finance; but most important of all in organisation."

However large commercial organisations seem now, their proportional scale at the turn of the century was greater still. When J. P. Morgan brokered the creation of US Steel in July 1901, it was capitalised at $us1.4 billion, while the whole of the American manufacturing was worth only $us9 billion. It employed 168,000, controlled 1600 km of rail, 112 ore carriers, produced 65 per cent of American steel and mined half its iron ore. Yet to call US Steel a corporation in the modern sense would be a misnomer: it was the holding company for an aggregation of entities and would be bedevilled for decades by its internal incoherence. In broad and simple terms, business and its leadership moved into the future in three iterations, embodied in three individuals: John D. Rockefeller, Henry Ford and Alfred Sloan.

A grab of elementary economics may be helpful here. Business knows two ways to expand. The first is horizontal combination: buying rivals to reduce competition. This became a vogue in America's depression of the 1870s, when railroads responded to excess capacity and deflation by forming industry associations and cartels to fix rates among themselves. Thus what is known colloquially as the rise of the all-powerful trust in the commercial affairs of the United States; thus, too, the emergence of John D. Rockefeller, in real terms still history's wealthiest individual. Rockefeller hailed from Cleveland, at the terminus of railroads stretching from Pennsylvania's newly opened Oil Regions. He was a trader in pork, grain and other staples who invested in a couple of refineries and a barrel-making operation, and who rather than peeling away to count his cash after his first fortune remained to make many more. Standard Oil, established in January 1870, assumed its name to emphasise its products' uniform quality, but it also set standards for business in management expertise and in minatory bulk.

Rampaging across the Oil Regions throughout the 1870s, Rockefeller "horizontally combined" about 90 per cent of America's refining capacity into a giant trust, consolidated by the Standard Oil Trust Agreement of January 1882. He then seized on what's now understood as the second method of business expansion: vertical integration, the acquisition of suppliers and customers to reduce costs. Standard moved from refining into distribution by buying pipelines, then tackled marketing and finally exploration. Perhaps no enterprise in history has been so self-contained. Because the only commercial men Rockefeller despised as much as bankers were brokers, Standard Oil was funded almost entirely from retained earnings. And as Rockefeller believed in "uncovering no surface unnecessarily", trust headquarters was an unmarked greystone building at 26 Broadway in Lower Manhattan — described chillingly in Thomas Lawson's period classic *Frenzied Finance*: "Solid as a prison, towering as a steeple, its cold and forbidding facade seems to rebuke the heedless levity of the passing crowd, and frown on the frivolity of the stray sunbeams which in the late afternoon played round its impassive cornices."

Rockefeller, however, proved himself a unique hybrid — in the words of his biographer, Ron Chernow, "both the instinctive first-generation entrepreneur who founds a company and the analytic second-generation manager who extends and develops it". Standard's executive committee convened daily at noon. Rockefeller left the head of the table to the group's oldest member, Charles Pratt, and favoured consensus: "Our general rule was to take no important action till all of us were convinced of its wisdom." Some controls were strict: all expenditures above $5000 and salary increases above $50 a month required top-level approval. But other matters were devolved to a group of sub-committees — transportation, production, pipelines, domestic trade, export trade, manufacturing, purchasing, case and can, cooperage and others — served by a permanent secretariat consisting of eleven staff departments. Standard Oil's management corps, Lawson thought, were as drilled and disciplined as an army: "Every Standard Oil man must wear the 'Standard Oil collar'. This collar is riveted to each one as he is taken into 'the band', and can only be removed with the head of the wearer." Rockefeller espoused a commercial creed of the utmost rationality — "Real efficiency in work comes from knowing your facts and building upon that sure foundation" – and Standard Oil was built in his own image. Even Rockefeller's muckraker nemesis Ida Tarbell had to admit, "There was not a lazy bone in the organisation, not an incompetent hand, nor a stupid head."

"Down with all tyrants!" shouts a character in Eugene O'Neill's *A Moon for the Misbegotten*. "Goddamn Standard Oil!" God, though, had nothing to do with the eventual eclipse of the Standard Oil and its trust brethren: rather it was Teddy Roosevelt, whose Bureau of Corporations in February **1902** took the first of forty-four anti-trust actions in his seven-year presidency. And still Roosevelt declined to throw the Gilded Age into reverse, restraining himself even amid his famous **1907** damnation of "the malefactors of great wealth" at the Gridiron Club: "I believe in corporations. They are indispensable instruments of our modern civilisation; but I believe that they should be so supervised and so regulated that they shall act for the interests of the community as a whole." In some respects, Roosevelt's trust-busters actually accelerated the creation of big enterprises: the only way to avoid being regarded as one of those sinister associations, cartels, trusts or holding companies was to consolidate completely – to become, in other words, a giant corporation.

To the drive for dominance would henceforward be harnessed an avidity for efficiency. That there might even be "one best way" to work was the *idée fixe* of an American statistician, Frederick Winslow Taylor, whose approach was to decompose a job into its simplest activities and reduce the time required by each. The stopwatch-toting Taylorist manager has been a bogey of liberals and trade unionists ever since, and *The Principles of Scientific Management* (**1911**) at times takes on an unsettlingly totalitarian tone: "In the past, man has been first. In the future the System must be first." But many agreed, and none more wholeheartedly than Detroit's pioneering car-maker Henry Ford. No scholar has linked Taylor and Ford directly – Taylor ridiculed Ford's "very cheaply and roughly made" Model T, while Ford's rudimentary education would have been challenged by Taylor's tangled prose – but they were cultural kin. Ford's notion of mass assembly-line production methods was labour divided and conquered. "Both Taylor and Ford raised production, cut costs – and reduced the judgement and skill needed by the average worker," says Robert Kanigel, Taylor's biographer. "After Ford and Taylor, most jobs needed less of everything – less brains, less muscle, less independence." They also produced more of everything. Highland Park, at which the assembly line was finally applied to the production of whole cars in October 1913, was seen by Rockefeller as "the industrial miracle of the age". By 1920, Ford was producing a car a minute; by 1925, a car every ten seconds.

Ford challenged the mores of commerce in another equally important way, by seeing advantage in what he could do rather than in the prevention of what others might. "I found that competition was supposed to be a menace and that a good manager circumvented his competitors by getting a monopoly through artificial means," recalled Ford. "The idea was that there were only a certain number of people who could buy and that it was necessary to get their trade ahead of someone else." Ford expanded his business, instead, by building the market. His stated objective was to build a car that "no man making a good salary will be unable to own and enjoy" – and from January 1914 he also provided the good salary by paying workers $5 a day. Ford disingenuously described his offer of two and a half times the going rate as "a plain act of social justice"; he was simply troubled by staff turnover and anxious about saboteurs damaging his precious machines. But the reasons mattered little: 10,000 stormed the gate clamouring for work the day after the policy was announced. Ford had at a stroke begotten his own customers. No single gesture in industrial history marked more clearly the transformation of an age of scarcity into one of abundance.

When Ford commissioned his River Rouge works after World War I – ninety-three buildings connected by 149 km of railroad and 43 km of conveyor belts employing 75,000 men – he appeared to have brought industry to a peak of vertically integrated perfection. It had its own power plant, iron forges, fabricating facilities – even its own paper mill. "If absolute completeness and perfect adaptation of means to end justify the word," said J. A. Spender, "they are in their own way works of art." Ford's *My Life and Work*, first published in 1923, was devoured by everyone from Konosuke Matsushita, Japan's first significant industrialist, to Bertrand Russell and Bernard Shaw. It went through thirty editions in Germany, where Hitler was an admirer, and became popular in Russia, where Lenin and Stalin championed "the teaching of the Taylor system and its systematic trial and adaptation".

Seldom, however, has a public figure trashed their reputation so conscientiously. Even overlooking the assembly line's dehumanising propensities – and Ford candidly conceded his conviction that "a great business is really too big to be human" – his deeds and dicta feature something to offend everybody, from his beastly maltreatment of his son and the prickly praetorian guard he maintained at River Rouge to his purse-mouthed disgust with shareholders and anti-Semitic outpourings in the *Dearborn Independent*. And, for all his genius as a manufacturer, Ford was an abject failure as a manager, abhorring all aspects of business bar production: "There is no bent of mind more dangerous than that which is described as the 'genius for organisation'. And so the Ford factories have no organisation, no specific duties attaching to any position, no line of succession or of authority." He steadily alienated his closest allies, sacked his ablest manufacturers and salesmen, and prohibited the most basic bureaucratic functions, one day capriciously firing all the company's accountants. "They're not productive," he railed. "They don't do any real work. I want them out of here today." The company became like a powerful engine harnessed to a driverless shell, for Ford also forbade any change to his dear but dour Model T. When he finally discontinued the marque in March 1927, he simply closed the factory, only then commencing design of its successor. John Kenneth Galbraith observed, "If there is any certainty as to what a businessman is, he is assuredly the things Ford was not." Alfred Sloan of Ford's great rival General Motors, by contrast, would be business's glass of fashion for fully half a century.

Alfred Sloan joined General Motors when his Hyatt Roller Bearing Company was acquired in July 1916. A holding company of automotive businesses gathered together by a charismatic but crazy-brave entrepreneur called William Durant, GM was at the time in more or less constant upheaval. Sloan's response, when Durant finally lost his job after an automotive market slump in September 1920, was to institute what Peter Drucker has called "the first deliberate attempt to organise the modern large industrial enterprise", combining Rockefeller's zeal for organisation with Ford's passion for production.

With Durant's successor, Pierre Du Pont, scion of the great chemicals firm, Sloan diagnosed GM's most recent prostration as the outcome of poor information. Output had been increased despite a six-month time lag on sales data, allowing inventory to blow out. Production schedules would henceforward be regularised by head office, based on figures from dealers collected every ten days and monthly information on car registrations. Sloan also believed in the most rigorous financial controls, and in January 1921 obtained from Du Pont Corporation an outstanding accountant, F. Donaldson Brown, who had dreamed up such exotic ideas as "turnover" and "return on investment". Applying these ideas at GM, Sloan coined the Nelsonian epigram, "Every dollar must make a showing for itself."

As he built this centre, Sloan proceeded more or less simultaneously with a scheme known as "decentralisation". As classically delineated by Nobel laureate Ronald Coase, the rationale for the large corporation is that combining activities in a single entity lowers "transactional costs": the expenses incurred in matching buyers and sellers, negotiating prices and finalising contracts. The problem is that large organisations also tend toward diseconomies of scale. There are agency costs, where the firm develops a stake in its own survival, and information costs, when managers lose track of what's happening. There is also the problem of the "free rider": the larger an organisation becomes, the greater the tendency for individuals to slacken off, failing to contribute their fair share to the common weal. The objective, then, is paradoxical: a corporation should be as big as it has to be, and as small as it can be.

Sloan resolved these tensions by envisioning a multi-divisional firm overlain by a head office controlling functions such as strategy, treasury and research, and reporting to executive and finance committees which answered in their turn to directors. "I do not regard size as a barrier," he asserted. "To me it is only a problem of management." In a memo that stands to management of the corporation as Luther's ninety-five theses do to the Reformation, Sloan contended that "decentralisation" would improve organisational morale "by placing each operation on its own foundation", permit the collection of financial data "correctly reflecting the relation between the net return and the invested capital of each operating division", and enable GM to "direct the placing of additional capital where it will result in the greatest benefit to the corporation as a whole". Sloan's idea wasn't entirely original: both Du Pont Corporation and Germany's Siemens had explored similar structures. But he was bolder. Where they were controlled by owner-managers, GM resembled the old Pennsylvania Railroad in being run by salarymen.

In his immersion in systems and structures, historian Thomas McCraw remarks, Sloan did for "human beings" what Ford had done for "physical machines". Demarcations between GM's car divisions, furthermore, were along product lines, each with a specific demographic in mind: "a car for every purse and purpose", in the famous formulation, with "Chevrolet for the *hoi polloi*, Pontiac for the poor but proud, Oldsmobile for the comfortable but discreet, Buick for the striving, Cadillac for the rich". GM, in Sloan's aphorism, did not make automobiles, but money.

Sloan was avowedly a leader, seeking explicitly "to centralise the control of all the executive functions of the corporation in the President as its chief executive officer". He later forced the resignations of Pierre Du Pont and executive committee member John Raskob when they joined the anti-prohibition movement, explaining that, "General Motors is not in politics. It will not permit its prestige, its organisation, or its property to be used for political purposes." But notice that "it": Sloan was also determined to de-personalise management, to create a firm that was not beholden to the impulses of a messianic individual, like a Durant or a Ford. When *Fortune* studied Sloan at work with his executives in August 1 9 3 8, he was no more than *primus inter pares*:

> In this committee work Mr Sloan displays an almost inhuman detachment from personalities, a human and infectious enthusiasm for the facts. Never in committee or out does he give an order in the ordinary sense, saying "I want you to do this." Rather he reviews the data and then sells an idea, pointing out what could be done. Brought to consider the facts in open discussion, all men, he feels, are on an equal footing. Management is no longer a matter of taking orders, but of taking counsel.

It was thirty years since Ambrose Bierce had defined a "corporation" as "an ingenious device for obtaining individual profit without individual responsibility". Sloan had now vindicated an earlier lexicographer, Dr Johnson, who believed that "wit can stand its ground against truth only a little while". The modern industrial corporation, consolidated into a single entity but redefined along divisional lines, run by a hierarchy of salaried managers reporting to a board and CEO, had arrived – and has never really left. If you can set aside any ideological *parti pris* for a moment, you might even salute it as the most important invention of the twentieth century. You might then wonder why in all likelihood you have not heard of Alfred Sloan. The straightforward answer is that much as we enjoy bandying round words like "capitalism" and "globalisation", we prefer to regard them as impersonal forces synonymous with exploitation rather than as the works of human individuals. But the other reason for Sloan's anonymity is that he sought it. GM eclipsed Ford's market share in 1 9 3 2 and never looked back. During World War II, its employee numbers grew to half a million, its sales to $us12 billion; a decade later it was the first corporation to net profits of more than $us1 billion. Yet

Sloan remained amazingly obscure: he left no private papers, says biographer David Farber, because "his life was so interwoven with GM that he couldn't separate his affairs from those of the corporation."

The effacement of the individual capitalist by the salaryman was also an Australian phenomenon. Where most companies had been controlled by their big shareholders in the nineteenth century, their daily affairs by the 1920s and 1930s were increasingly the preserve of professional managers. And without big, greedy, meddlesome owners looking over their shoulders, the likes of Essington Lewis, W. S. Robinson, Colin Fraser and Herbert Gepp found increasing scope for their talents: when Lewis dissuaded BHP's board from installing the costly Duplex steel-making system in February 1921, he was also striking a blow for executive expertise. Like Sloan, Lewis cared little for appearances. When promoted to BHP's board with the title of managing director five years later, Geoffrey Blainey has noted, Lewis "shunned the glitter that went with the power; he simply demanded the power".

That widened separation of ownership and control, essentially unavoidable since limited liability, was accelerated by industry's growing scale. Long a feature of American capitalism, the merger spread to Europe: the chemical giants Bayer, Hoechst and BASF formed IG Farbenindustrie in 1925; a host of German steel companies became Vereinigte Stahlwerke in 1926. Britain's Imperial Chemical Industries was created in a four-way merger the same year, Distillers Company in a six-way merger the following year, and Unilever and Metal Box in other combinations two years later. Australia followed a similar path. Australian Paper & Pulp formed Amcor's forerunner Australian Paper Mills in September 1926 by acquiring its rivals Cumberland and Commonwealth Paper Board; Dunlop absorbed Perdriau Rubber and Barnet Glass in April 1929; Holden was pocketed by GM in March 1931; BHP effortlessly enfolded Australian Iron & Steel in October 1935.

Grown so large as to outstrip the capacities of solitary capitalists and even syndicates of investors to own them, corporations were taking on lives of their own. "The deindividualisation of ownership simultaneously implies the objectification of the thing owned," said Walter Rathenau, son of and successor to the founder of German electrical giant AEG. "The claims to ownership are subdivided in such a fashion, and are so mobile, that the enterprise assumes an independent life, as if it belonged to no one." His words were truer than he knew: his death from an assassin's bullet in 1922 ended family influence at the firm. Fortune magazine, founded in January 1930, tended to publish "muscular stories about muscular industries": steel, coal, manufacturing. The individual nominally in charge, where he appeared at all, was an afterthought: by 1938, the average American CEO held just 0.3 per cent of his company's shares.

Alfred Sloan was unusual. Having swapped his Hyatt shares for scrip, he was a sizeable GM shareholder. Yet he saw that role as secondary: "Naturally I like to see GM stock register a good price on the market, but that is just a matter of pride. Personally I consider its price fluctuations inconsequential. What has counted with me is the true value of the property as a business, as an opportunity for the exercise of management talent." Or lack of talent, as the case might be. For the Sloanist corporation soon attracted critics. The atomisation of ownership, Adolf Berle and Gardiner Means warned darkly in The Modern Corporation and Private Property (1932), meant that "the men in control of a corporation can operate in their own interests, and can divest a portion of the asset fund of income stream to their own uses, such is their privilege." The lapsed Trotskyist James Burnham, who gave the phenomenon a name in The Managerial Revolution (1940), predicted a kind of socialism by stealth: "In the new structure, when its foundations are completed, there will be no capitalists." A young economist, Peter Drucker, whom GM invited to study its methods, sounded a reproachful note in his Concept of the Corporation (1946): because "in every large organisation there is a natural tendency to discourage initiative and to put a premium on conformity", big business was destined to suffer "from parochialism of the executive imagination".

Yet no one could doubt the profundity of Sloan's influence. It is instanced by another first to his credit: he was the first CEO to appear on *Fortune*'s cover. What's notable about this, given that business magazines now rely on CEOs as *Vanity Fair* relies on sleek-headed stars and *Vogue* on airbrushed models, is that it did not happen until September 1963. Even then, the portrait of a pensive Sloan was not to celebrate him as a super-man but to promote a serialisation of his *My Years with General Motors* – a work as bloodless as its appendices, with their column upon column of numbers and page after page of schematic diagrams documenting GM's financial performance and multi-divisional structure. It was, as Drucker observed, "perhaps the most impersonal book of memoirs ever written – and this was clearly intentional".

A startling aspect of the cult of the CEO, then, is how recent it is. For much of the century, those nominally in charge of corporations have bare-ly been known. In the 1950s, the facelessness of corporate America was a theme beloved of social critics. When the CEO appeared in movies, he was in thrall to systems that had cost him either his humanity or his vision. In *Patterns* (1956), conniving boss Walter Ramsey (Everett Sloane) hires bright young Fred Staples (Van Heflin) in order to marginalise, then dispose of, dim but loyal William Briggs (Ed Begley). In *The Man in the Gray Flannel Suit* (1956), the more benevolent Ralph Hopkins (Fredric March) takes a kindly interest in speechwriter Tom Rath (Gregory Peck), but in his personal sadness suggests to Rath how not to live his life. Even in gen-erally positive portraits, corporate hierarchies seemed to militate against the rise of the best. When Tredway Corporation's hard-driving CEO Avery Bullard dies in the opening reel of *Executive Suite* (1954), his design chief, Don Walling (William Holden), mourns: "He was a great man. The greatest man I've ever known." But Walling, while clearly the outstanding candidate, wants no part of boardroom bloodletting. "I'm not going to die young at the top of the tower worrying about bond issues," he assures his wife. "I'm a designer, not a politician." When Walling is finally per-suaded to seek promotion, it is to restore Tredway's old sense of mission:

Bullard, he decides, had built a great company but "finally lost sight of why he was building it – why he was the man he was".

Not surprisingly, CEOs jibbed at the criticism. US Steel's Benjamin Fairless thought there was a certain nobility in anonymity: "America is full of successful people you never heard of. Men and women whom fame passed by." Du Pont's Crawford Greenewalt believed that, "The more effective an executive, the more his own identity and personality blend into the background of his organisation." And America Inc. was flourishing, in verifiable ways. Even in the fleeting recession of 1957, the hundred largest corporations all made profits, and would until 1964. But the controls of Sloanism were steadily becoming rigidities. For all his faith in "executive talent", Alfred Sloan had believed in specialised technical expertise. "I happen to be of the old school", he explained, "who thinks that a knowledge of the business is essential to a successful administration." By the time he expressed this view, however, it *was* an "old school" way of thinking. Business-school degrees were increasingly standing in for experience, management accounting systems for direct acquaintance with products and markets.

In some respects, the most influential group of businessmen immediately after the war were the Whiz Kids: ten US Army Air Corps statisticians marshalled by Colonel Tex Thornton who sold themselves and their process control methods to Henry Ford II. Ford, by this stage, was legendary for its chaos – in one department, it's said, expenses were estimated by weighing invoices. The Whiz Kids, who included a virtuoso financial controller Ed Lundy and future company presidents Arjay Miller and Robert McNamara, changed all that. Junior salesman Lee Iacocca recalled, "In the days before computers, these guys *were* the computers." With his back-combed hair and rimless glasses, McNamara struck contemporaries as the technocrat supreme – "the first incarnation of the modern professional manager", says David Halberstam. His feeling for product was minimal. He once visited Ford's great designer Don Frey with a set of statistics, weights and costs for a new car. Frey asked eagerly, "Do you want a soft car, a hot, sexy car, a comfortable car, a car for the young, or a car for the middle class? Whose car is it? What does it feel like?" McNamara looked blankly back: "That's very interesting. Write down what you think is right." About Ford's business as business, however, McNamara was possessed of total knowledge and total confidence – a confidence he also exhibited as secretary of defence during the Vietnam War, then as chief of the World Bank. "The real threat to democracy", he said, "comes not from over-management but under-management."

A typical transition was Chrysler's. GM alumnus Walter Chrysler had stamped his name on the company in the 1920s with a string of outstanding vehicles, including the DeSoto and the Plymouth. "There is in manufacturing a creative job that only poets are supposed to know," he said. "Someday I'd like to show a poet how it feels to design and build a locomotive." But after his death in August 1940, the company lost its way, failing to introduce a new model for eleven years. Finally, in 1961, Chrysler sought safety in numbers, as it were, appointing an accountant as CEO, Lynn Townsend. Chrysler chairman George Love celebrated Townsend precisely because he knew little about the automotive business:

> He is the right man because he is figure-minded. It used to be possible to control the company through personal contact. But when a company gets this big, you no longer know all the people. You can't see that so-and-so is loafing. So you need a man for whom figures live. You control the company by a knowledge of figures. Townsend can spot trouble through them.

Accounting historians H. Thomas Johnson and Robert S. Kaplan conjecture that this trend had been almost forty years in the making: "Until the 1920s, managers invariably relied on information about the underlying processes, transactions and events that produce financial numbers. By the 1960s and 1970s, however, managers commonly relied on the financial numbers alone." And for managerial capitalism, this rationalist view of the corporation would come to have some ironic implications.

The concept of the conglomerate was simple and radical. A range of businesses beneath the same organisational roof but following different economic cycles should be inured from exogenous economic shocks. Better still, a CEO should be able to optimise capital deployment by stripping surpluses from one constituent to bestow on another. The conglomerate, then, redefined expansion. Rather than growing by horizontal combination or vertical integration, this was growth by diversification: the acquisition of undertakings unrelated to previous activities, blended into the whole by common financial controls. And in this way did the conglomerate redefine the function of CEO: mere stewards no longer, they were recast as capitalists, building companies not from new products or superior services, but from other companies run by people like themselves.

Perhaps the most successful – and sinister – *conglomerateur* was Harold Geneen, of whom it was said that "the g is soft, as in Jesus, not hard, as in God". ITT, a lacklustre collection of American telephone companies with annual sales of less than $us1 million when he became its CEO in 1959, acquired 275 companies in two decades, from Avis and Sheraton Hotels to Aetna Finance and Hartford Insurance. Geneen was all-seeing, all-knowing and would have been all-doing "if I had enough arms and legs". As it was, he kept the managers of a workforce that grew to 350,000 in a state of exhilarated terror, presiding over 200 days of meetings a year in unflagging pursuit of the "cold, hard facts". It was said that he could sit for twelve hours, was accompanied on trips by as many as fourteen briefcases; certainly he inspired scores of imitators, such as Peter Grace of W. R. Grace, so fervently of the faith that "numbers are reality" that he pasted spreadsheets in the corridors of hotels in which he resided, and Charles Bluhdorn, whose Gulf & Western was the model for Engulf & Devour in Mel Brooks' *Silent Movie*.

As quickly as conglomerates came into fashion so they went: groups became so diverse as to make meaningful profit targets unascertainable, competition for capital unmanageable, and accounts unintelligible. But the "Go-Go Years" echoed loud and long. Egged on by the emergent management consulting industry, bosses everywhere were encouraged to reconceive their businesses as portfolios: the matrix designed by Bruce Henderson of Boston Consulting Group, which divided businesses into stars, cash cows, dogs and "question marks", became history's most ubiquitous management tool. Diversification was smart. Diversification was fun. Why give money to shareholders when you could be spending it yourself? Mergers and acquisitions in the US grew from 2000 in 1965 to 6000 in 1969 as even industry giants became mini-conglomerates. Gulf Oil bid for the Ringling Bros and Barnum & Bailey Circuses. British cement manufacturer Blue Circle acquired lawnmower-maker Qualcast on the strategic principle that "your garden is next to your house". Australia's Dunlop "began to go Christmas shopping throughout the year", acquiring dozens of ill-assorted businesses, some bought and sold within months, and almost buckled beneath their weight.

Such strains were not uncommon. The first attempt by CEOs to modify their corporations was largely fruitless. Harvard's Michael Porter has claimed that three-quarters of diversifications at big American companies between 1950 and 1986 were unwound or sold. In explaining this collective failure of managerial capitalism, economists saw a recrudescence of the principal/agent problem, that separation of ownership and control made manifest in *Dombey & Son*. According to agency theory, managers resist distributing cash to shareholders because cash reserves increase their autonomy, and because spending on acquisitions increases the size of their company and thus their compensation. Like most theories it contains both truth and a host of exceptions and qualifications: there are despotic principals and rational agents, just as there are benign owners and self-interested managers. But what's curious is that the greatest beneficiary of the unwinding of the trend to diversification would be those who had squandered the most money: CEOs.

After the Go-Go Years came the Slow-Go Years. As Sloan's *My Years with General Motors* was the canonical work of his generation, Pontiac boss John DeLorean's *On a Clear Day You Can See General Motors*, published in 1979, became the key text of his, lampooning corporate conformity; one typical anecdote concerned GM vice-chairman Richard Terrell playing Tweedledee to chairman Richard Gerstenberg's Tweedledum:

> The dialogue would go something like this. Gerstenberg: "God-damnit. We cannot afford any new models next year because of the cost of this federally mandated equipment. There is no goddamn money left for styling changes. That's the biggest problem we face."
>
> Terrell, after about ten minutes: "Dick, Goddamnit, we've just got to face up to the fact that the biggest problem we face is the cost of this federally mandated equipment. This stuff costs so much that we just don't have any money left for styling our new cars. That's our biggest problem."
>
> Gerstenberg: "You're Goddamn right, Dick. That's a good point."

By now, too, it was emerging that American bosses ritually spent more time on points than products. There'd been no real revision of shop-floor practices since the Taylorist "scientific management" revolution, which unions had steadily turned to their members' advantage by imposing stark demarcations between jobs and responsibilities. On pilgrimages to Detroit from the 1950s onwards, Japanese automotive executives like Toyota's Kiichiro Toyoda and Taiichi Ohno were awed and appalled by the amount of *muda* – wasted effort, wasted value, wasted time. Because their small domestic market precluded long production runs and extreme specialisation of labour, the Japanese approached manufacturing far more frugally and fastidiously. As American businesses scrambled to assimilate *kaizen*, *kanban* cards, PDCA cycles and *pokayoke* devices in the 1970s, their confidence took a severe knock. Generally, the larger the industry, the less prepared it was for the *tsunami* of economic rivalry. Suddenly the CEO was on the defensive. Never mind *The Stepford Wives* (1972), what about those Stepford husbands? How could one believe in bosses like those nominally directing the inert insurance giant in Joseph Heller's *Something Happened* (1974), as seen through the eyes of the novel's chief protagonist, junior executive Bob Slocum:

> All these twelve men are elderly now and drained by time and success of energy and ambition. Many have spent their whole lives here. They seem friendly, slow and content when I come across them in the halls (they seem dead) and are always courteous and mute when they ride with others in the public elevators. They no longer work hard. They hold meetings, make promotions, and allow their names to be used on announcements that are prepared and issued by somebody else. Nobody is sure anymore who really runs the company.

Among the great corporations hardest hit by economic austerity was Chrysler, whose market share nearly halved and whose stock shed four-fifths of its value during the 1970s. No organisation was riper for regeneration, and no one better credentialled to lead it than Ford's Lee Iacocca – the first business chieftain since the days of Rockefeller and Ford whose reputation would come to rival that of his company.

A skilful salesman, Iacocca's most successful promotion had been of himself in 1964, when he'd claimed credit for the sporty, spunky Mustang. Not that he'd dreamed it, designed it or even named it. His contribution to its creation was smuggling it past Ford's querulous bureaucrats, board and boss – which landed him on the covers of *Time* and *Newsweek* in the same week and earned him the undying enmity of Henry Ford II, who finally sacked him with the tart explanation, "I just don't like you."

When Iacocca joined it in September 1979, Chrysler was poised to default on debts of $us4.75 billion. He persuaded its 400 banks to forgive $us1.1 billion in return for preferred stock, and the US government to guarantee another $us1.2 billion. But Iacocca's chief triumph, as with the Mustang, was in putting a face on the company – his own. He endorsed newspaper ads – "Would America Be Better Off

Without Chrysler?" – defending the government bail-out. He appeared in the first of eighty television commercials spruiking a money-back guarantee if people disliked their new Chryslers. He identified with popular, patriotic causes, including a charity to refurbish the Statue of Liberty. *Fortune* slapped him on its cover in August 1 9 8 0, peering through a clapperboard, with the headline, "The Boss as Pitchman". The pitch? "I'm here. I'm real and I'm responsible for this company. And to show that I mean it, I'm signing on the dotted line."

Chrysler's revival – based partly on productivity gains, partly on debt relief and rather a lot on using tariff advantages to raise prices rather than reduce costs – could hardly proceed quickly enough. Iacocca seemed to follow not so much a strategy document as a script. No sooner had Chrysler returned to profitability in the second quarter of 1 9 8 2 than he was pressing aides to promote him:

> As other accolades poured in, the cover of *Time* became an obsession. He spoke constantly of men he knew in the publishing world who said they could help fix it for him. *Time*, however, sceptical as to whether the Chrysler rebound would last, hesitated. When John DeLorean was arrested in a drug bust in the fall of 1 9 8 2, and *Time* put him on the cover, Iacocca was enraged. "Here I've saved this goddamn company and I can't get on the cover of *Time*," he said, "and that son-of-a-bitch DeLorean gets caught dealing drugs and he makes it. What the hell is wrong with these people?"

When it finally featured him in March 1 9 8 3 – "America Loves Listening to Lee" – *Time* specifically bruited Iacocca's presidential ambitions. The only disincentive, it seemed, was that America's social problems were too tractable: "Running Chrysler has been a bigger job than running the country. I could handle the national economy in six months." The more prosaic reason was the fortune Iacocca was making, harvesting $us43 million from an equity-based compensation scheme over six years, and selling seven million copies of his autobiography. "No matter what you have, it's never enough," he once said, and grabbed every perquisite within reach.

Revisionists have since depicted Iacocca as a tyrant petty in all things save pay, claiming credit for every success, blaming Japan, OPEC or the US government for every setback, and playing off potential successors to prolong his reign; before finally yielding to Bob Eaton in January 1992, the name Iacocca was reputed to stand for "I am chairman of Chrysler Corporation always". But it was the manner of Iacocca's reign rather than its methods, or even its outcomes, that proved culturally formative. Though ultimately just another salaried executive, Iacocca swaggered like one of America's self-made capitalists of yore.

By opting to take much of his remuneration in the form of stock, Iacocca also signed up to a popular new doctrine espoused by an accounting professor from Northwestern University, Alfred Rappaport. In a far-reaching paper in *Harvard Business Review* – "Selecting Strategies That Create Shareholder Value" – Rappaport scorned time-honoured accounting devices for pricing business activities based on earnings and asset backing. He promoted instead a metric based on discounted cash flow: essentially what someone should be willing to pay today in order to receive anticipated cash flow in future years, based on a company's free cash flows discounted by the weighted average of its cost of capital. "Cash is a fact," observed Rappaport. "Profit is an opinion."

A phrase much over-used, even abused, in the years since, the "shareholder value" concept was at the time revelatory. In terms of discounted cash flow, many corporations, especially those still hypertrophic from diversification binges in the 1960s and 1970s, could be seen as cheap – obtaining them the attentions of marauders like Carl Icahn and Ron Perelman in the US, Britons Lord Hanson and Sir James Goldsmith, and Australians Robert Holmes a Court and Alan Bond. Market forces helped: the quest at investment banks and brokers for new sources of fee income, and a global bull market in equities which commenced in August 1982. But this was also a cultural shift, reflecting a tide of opinion in favour of deregulation, tolerant of debt, aching for change, yet nostalgic for old-fashioned entrepreneurship. In the most famous scene in Oliver Stone's *Wall Street* (1 9 8 7), the proxy fight at the annual meeting of Teldar Paper, the archetypal raider Gordon Gekko (Michael Douglas) portrays himself as incarnating a prelapsarian, anti-Sloanist golden age of American capitalism:

> Now, in the days of the free market when our country was a top industrial power, there was accountability. The Carnegies, the Mellons, the men who built this great industrial empire made sure there was, because it was their money at stake. Today, management has no stake in the company. Altogether those men sitting up there own less than 3 per cent of the company. You own the company and you're being royally screwed by these bureaucrats with their stock lunches, their hunting and fishing trips, their corporate jets and their golden parachutes.

Homing in on the wastefulness of agents without the economic interest of the principal, the raiders seemed to score a powerful philosophical point, especially to those with recollections of the diversification mania of the 1 9 6 0s. And even when bosses did have their money on the line, "shareholder value" was a popular rallying-cry. The climactic proxy fight in Norman Jewison's 1 9 9 1 film *Other People's Money* pits "Jorgy" Jorgenson, octogenarian patriarch of New England Cable & Wire, against wily wheeler-dealer Larry Garfield – with an unexpected twist. Jorgenson (played with rumpled integrity by Gregory Peck) pleads with shareholders to resist Garfield's predations: "Take a look around. Look at your neighbour. You won't kill him. That's called murder and it's illegal. Well, this too is murder. On a mass scale. Except on Wall Street, they call it 'maximising shareholder value'." But "Larry the Liquidator" (a bouncy, bug-eyed Danny De Vito) believes that the murder has already occurred; he's just claiming the insurance, and distributing it to investors: "I'm not your *best* friend. I'm your *only* friend. I don't make anything? I'm making *you* money. And, lest we forget, that's the only reason any of you became shareholders in the first place." And the figure who turns the result Garfield's way? The company's self-serving CEO, Bill Coles (a sleazy Dean Jones), who's turned over his votes because Jorgenson has denied him a golden parachute: "Lord of the manor. House on the hill. Said he didn't want to talk about a funeral when there wasn't a corpse."

And by this time, CEOs were fighting back. Leery of "shareholder value" at first, they had discovered the attractions of the takeover market themselves, in particular that popular variant, the leveraged buy-out (where the assets of the target company were used as collateral for extremely heavy borrowings). A CEO was the ideal leader of such a deal. "If you get the right general," said an executive at the buy-out giant Kohlberg Kravis Roberts, "the colonels and lieutenants will fall in line." Their involvement also obtained the imprimatur of academics like Harvard's Michael Jensen, who had been urging for many years that bosses be paid in equity, to "align" their interests with those of investors, while their minds were concentrated by large quantities of debt, to prevent their misuse of retained earnings on acquisitions and creature comforts. So CEOs joined the Gadarene rush to privatise, re-structure and re-float public companies – between **1980** and **1989** there were **2385** deals in the US worth **$us245** billion – and usually made a killing. Perversely, in fact, top management often benefited from its earlier inefficiency: the fat they'd marbled into their corporations could be boiled away to lighten debt.

Not every buy-out ended happily ever after. Australia's biggest – John Elliott's attempt to secure control of Elders IXL for his coterie – finished in ruin and recrimination. But, by the early **1990**s, when just about every corporation seemed to have been downsized, rightsized or excised, CEOs had never been wealthier or, thanks to legal ramparts erected to ward raiders off, cosier. As a character exclaimed in David Lodge's **1988** novel *Nice Work*, it was a "Brave New World where only the managing directors have jobs". Some CEOs seemed unusually keen to keep it that way. *Fortune* 500 companies eliminated **3.2** million jobs in the name of "shareholder value" over the decade – the **$us1** trillion in takeover debt had to be paid for somehow – and their blood-letting was emulated round the world. Robert Horton's austere administration at BP inspired among his subordinates the abbreviation BOHICA: "Bend Over Here It Comes Again". Europe's most admired boss Percy Barnevik, who ran engineering giant ABB, believed that "you can go into any traditionally centralised corporation and cut its headquarters staff by 90 per cent in a year." Even in Australian executive ranks, less was considered more. "There was something gruesome in a corporate sort of way", wrote former State Bank of NSW treasurer Graham Hand, "about highly paid senior executives discussing the job losses of their former colleagues as if they were personal achievements."

That wasn't all there was to the American *risorgimento* in the 1980s. CEOs of a new entrepreneurial wave in information technology owed nothing to debt or downsizing, and fitted no identikit, new or old. When *Time* selected Apple's Steve Jobs as its Man of the Year in 1982, its reporter found him so obnoxious that the personal computer was substituted to become "Machine of the Year" instead. When Jobs' compadre Larry Ellison consented to a study of Oracle Corporation, it was entitled *The Difference between God and Larry Ellison*: the reason – prepare to be amazed – is that God doesn't think he's Larry Ellison. Their mutual nemesis, meanwhile, first featured on *Fortune*'s cover in July 1986: begoggled Bill Gates, a thirty-year-old Harvard drop-out, had just earned $US350 million in the float of Microsoft. He has since been back on the cover two-dozen times, while expanding his personal wealth almost 150-fold.

Silicon Valley offered succour to those who saw owners as inherently superior to mere managers. But, since emulating Microsoft was scarcely an alternative for most businesses, a self-styled "lousy, grungy engineer" called Jack Welch would exert greater influence on the mores.

General Electric's top job has been described as the "corporate equivalent of the American presidency". Welch's predecessor, Reg Jones, had been his generation's favourite CEO, who spoke of "working with the grain" and sheltering management from "the financial community and the owners of the enterprise". When Jack Welch took over in April

1981, he inverted this order of precedence, running the shareholder-value standard to the top of the flagpole. His demand that GE be the biggest or second-biggest competitor in its every activity entailed asset disposals worth $us9 billion, acquisitions worth $us18 billion, compacting a 29-tier wedding cake of managers into a simpler five-layer sponge, and the elimination of 111,000 jobs in five years. The 5000 per cent appreciation in GE's stock price over Welch's twenty-year tenure mattered for a simple reason. Its changes were not about fixing an old corporation, as Iacocca had, or building a new one, like Gates was: they were crisis management without the crisis. To business, Welch became a kind of folk hero. Even his tart nickname "Neutron Jack", bestowed by *Newsweek* in January 1982 for the way his policies eliminated people and preserved buildings, became a term of endearment (DaimlerChrysler's Jürgen Schrempp now proudly wears the handle "Neutron Jürgen"). More or less every CEO since has sought a little of Welch's magic: Enron was so eager to promote Jeff Skilling as "a younger, cooler Jack Welch" that they head-hunted his GE publicist.

Time's "Greatest Businessman of the Twentieth Century" has had his share of luck. Much of GE's success could be ascribed to a structure arrived at almost inadvertently, where its old industrial businesses reposed alongside newer activities in commercial and consumer lending, leasing and insurance. With GE Industrial's triple-A credit rating underwriting GE Capital's more profitable activities, GE became a financial business trading with the risk premium of an industrial blue chip. And as for working out Welch's business philosophy ... well, it's hard. The GE way, management theorist fans maintain, is inculcated at its famous Crotonville conference centre. Noel Tichy has described GE's "Work-Out" sessions in "The Pit" – where groups of 40–100 employees share views on their businesses, bosses and bureaucracies – as a vestige of the frontier spirit: "These touchy-feely, egalitarian methods may strike people from other countries as peculiarly, perhaps even laughably, American. Without question they are rooted in American culture."

Under Welch, though, GE was also imperial: his flattening of GE's management, to borrow Anthony Sampson's words, "replaced a republic with a monarchy". For all GE's egalitarian get-up-and-go, for example, it only responded to the internet in 1999, long after most companies, when Welch wondered why his wife was spending so much time pecking at her laptop. "Since GE had excellent managers who were supposedly free to share ideas and opinions," Jeff Madrick observed, "it seems odd that the company did not undertake a major e-business program until the idea dawned on Welch himself." And in many of its doings, Welch's GE seems to have been as "touchy-feely" as a regiment of Gurkhas. Annual rank-and-yank performance reviews isolated and proscribed an underclass of 10 per cent, who were axed if they failed to improve. "Some think it's cruel or brutal to remove the bottom 10 per cent," Welch has stated defiantly. "It isn't. It's just the opposite."

Welch's autobiography, *Straight from the Gut*, is appropriately visceral. On the subject of acquisitions, the idea seems to make good ones (like RCA in December 1985), not bad ones (like Kidder Peabody in April 1986). On the subject of initiative, you should allow plenty of it (to the likes of NBC chief Bob Wright) except when you shouldn't (to anyone like rogue fixed-income trader Joseph Jett, revealed in April 1994 to have confected $us350 million "profits"). Even ego is a flexible concept to Welch, cringingly modest in describing his methods ("I hate having to use the first person"), defiantly avaricious in defending his rewards ("I earned what I got … I gave it all I had"). Welch effectively enjoins imitators not to "do as I do", or even "do as I say", but "be as I am". Want corporate performance like GE? Hire someone like Jack Welch. And pay him a bomb.

So how much should a CEO be paid? Such a question has been circulating since Plato told Aristotle that no one should receive more than five times the wages of the lowest-paid worker. And just as Catholic theologians in the Middle Ages were obsessed with the doctrine of "just price" – divine justification for why one type of labour commanded greater rewards than another – businessmen have sought their own laws. J. P. Morgan decreed that the highest of his men should earn no more than twenty times as much as the humblest – a ratio Peter Drucker also recommended more recently. But such calculations have tended to make matters more arbitrary rather than less.

Executive pay first complicated about seventy years ago when performance bonuses came into vogue. They pass without comment now, but are a curious concept: one receives a salary for doing one's job and, after some occult calculus, a bonus for doing it well, as though excellence and endeavour were not factored into preliminary estimates. They certainly puzzled their initial recipients. When a 1930 stockholder suit investigated his $US1.5 million *baksheesh*, Bethlehem Steel president Eugene Grace stated confidently, "The factor used to determine my bonus is 1.5 per cent." A lawyer asked, "1.5 per cent of what?" Grace paused, then conceded, "I don't know."

Still more curious was the concept of the golden parachute – a payment to which an executive became entitled on the termination of an employment contract, usually in the event of a change of control. They began billowing in the late 1970s, as CEOs sought soft landings amid so much takeover turbulence; they were rationalised, indeed, as a way of discouraging the incumbent management from warding off bids merely to save their own skins, depriving shareholders in the process. Disinterested self-sacrifice, of course, was not the only behaviour they rewarded; as agreed payments on severance for whatever reason turned into a contractual norm, golden parachutes became, in some instances, a kind of bonus bestowed for failure. Britain's leading management writer, Charles Handy, observed that big valedictory payouts had made ineptitude as a senior executive the shortest route to instant millionairehood. Renegade compensation consultant Graef Crystal thought they should be designated "golden condoms", because "they protect the executive and screw the shareholders". Some golden parachutes even came equipped with golden cushions to land on, in the form of consultancy deals and retirement privileges. Paul Sticht of RJR Nabisco was said by his successor, Tylee Wilson, to be the company's sexual consultant: "When I want his fucking advice I'll ask for it."

CEO compensation began its 1990s inflation, however, not because CEOs were felt to deserve more, but because it was believed that they should be paid differently – to redress that abiding divergence of interests between those who ran and owned corporations. The philosophy was encapsulated in the title of one of Michael Jensen's influential articles: "It's Not How Much You Pay, But How". Management buy-outs were seen to have revived the entrepreneurial spirit, but their vice was that executives often ended up with personal wealth in illiquid, undiversified lumps.

Stock options – instruments granted by a company convertible into shares at a fixed price, thus allowing their acquisition on advantageous terms when the shares appreciate – first found favour in the US in 1950 because of their preferential capital gains tax treatment. They were initially treated with circumspection. IBM introduced a program in 1956, for example, but limited it to a few executives, and boss Tom Watson Jnr withdrew after two years. "We don't want to look like pigs," agreed financial controller Al Williams. A virtue of stock options, though, was that piggishness only burdened one's conscience. The Accounting Principles Board had solicited several learned papers from experts on their optimal costing, then when the responses proved irreconcilable arbitrarily assigned stock options a zero value. A chestnut of business is the free lunch's non-existence; here was a lunch not only free, but self-service and all-you-can-eat. Unlike a cash bonus or a parcel of free shares, both of which had to be peeled from the bottom line, the only cost of granting stock options that were then exercised and the shares sold was a slight dilution of the company's equity base. There was even a tax deduction.

Of course, stock options *do* have value. Which is why CEOs scramble after them. Which is why Jack Welch retired in December 2001 with $250 million in exercisable stock options and another $228 million in stock (aside from years of basic salary, bonuses and shares sold along the way, plus retirement perks with a capital value of $us73 million). Which is why Welch once jested that CEOs should never appoint academics to run their compensation committees: professors are more susceptible to envy than your average rich old man. Which is why Welch used them with such abandon: by 2000, more than 30,000 GE employees held options valued at $us12 billion, including Jerry Seinfeld (rewarded for a final series of his NBC comedy). Which is why GE is often credited with reinventing remuneration as a virtuous circle: give executives and employees access to the shareholder value they create, it is said, and they will create more. The company, what's more, doesn't pay – the market does. Presto! You've outsourced your payroll.

Of course, there's a catch; in fact, several. For one, stock option schemes cannot distinguish between how much of a share price's fizz is the recipient's doing, and how much is simply a market's overall effervescence. A broad rise in equity values is essential to any remuneration based on stock, but the rise should not be so steep that making money is as easy as falling off a log. Which, we know now, is what happened. In 1978, Disney CEO Cardon Walker earned $us1.5 million. Twenty years later, Disney CEO Michael Eisner took home $us575.6 million, mostly from options, and was one of five American CEOs splitting $us1.2 billion between them.

The imprecision is exacerbated by the stock option's quirky status as the neutrino of accounting: neither weight nor mass, but effect. Those who do not charge earnings for the cost of an economic benefit are apt to imagine that the benefit has no cost, and to distribute too much too liberally. Which, again, is what happened. Many companies began issuing options "at-the-money" (i.e. based on the current price of ordinary securities) with an automatic "reload" (i.e. replacements were issued every time options were exercised) but without any mechanisms for filtering general market rises or restricting the extent of cashing out. Some Silicon Valley plans resembled huge one-ticket lotteries. In May 2000, Apple awarded Steve Jobs a package that would be worth $us550 million if its stock rose 5 per cent a year over the next decade. Oracle responded by awarding Ellison twenty million options worth $us400 million, though he already owned 700 million Oracle shares. In Australia, thanks to an option plan in which the only performance hurdle was that shareholder return based on price and dividends exceed 10 per cent per annum compounded, Peter Smedley made $a20 million on bundling up and flogging the financial conglomerate Colonial.

Options, too, are notoriously seductive. They have no downside. If the price of ordinary securities falls below the option strike, the option's nominal value is the only cost. But if the price of ordinary shares rises, the benefits flow in plenty. When a share price fall is so unimportant, and a rise so remunerative, does there not exist a incitement to risk, even to recklessness? Which, very obviously, is what happened. Remember: the objective of granting top management equity was to mitigate the principal/agent problem, to make them think like owners. Instead it conferred all ownership's rewards while inuring them from all its risks. A brilliant incentive – for recipients.

For CEOs, the only disconcerting aspect to their booty was that restive shareholders might expect them to earn it. This began happening. In the 1980s, institutional investors notified CEOs of their dissatisfaction simply – they sold, and if enough shares changed hands, so did your company. By the 1990s, this had become less straightforward: with an increasing proportion of investment capital in so-called index funds, where holdings were weighted according to the proportion that a company represented of its market sector, portfolio managers faced what's been christened "the plight of the eternal shareholder". The question arose: if investment in many companies was more or less mandatory, could investors have a say in how these companies were run?

California Public Employees' Retirement System (CalPERS) was one of the first institutional investors to think so. After becoming boss of CalPERS in July 1987, Dale Hanson took careful aim at General Motors, by now a symbol both of American industrial pride and faded grandeur. GM chief Robert Stempel was hounded to his departure in October 1992 after announcing a $us4.45 billion loss. When investor insurrections soon after toppled three other top CEOs – American Express's James Robinson III, Westinghouse's Paul Lego, and IBM's John Akers – *Fortune's* cover story "The King Is Dead" forecast the end of "the imperial CEO". Big shareholders were soon making their presence felt everywhere, while small shareholders began marching into annual meetings like the Munchkins advancing on Emerald City to have it out with the Wizard of Oz. Even Australia's traditionally quiescent investors began acting up, notably at Westpac, where the resignation of chairman Sir Eric Neal and four directors in October 1992 was followed three months later by the sacking of managing director Frank Conroy and an unruly eight-hour annual meeting.

Ultimately, however, the dividends of shareholder activism have failed to match the financial and intellectual investments. In "The Promise of the Governed Corporation", John Pound boldly likened corporate governance to the "democratic political system", proposing that big shareholders be permitted to speak directly to senior managers and the board about what they think of policies and decisions. But this, as corporate governance expert Ira Millstein has conceded, is impractical: "Boards and certainly shareholders don't have the information to run the business. And they never will have without becoming managers themselves." CalPERS is the biggest American fund manager, controlling funds worth $us130 billion, but even it finds activism hard to justify in anything other than extreme cases because it is expensive and its rewards accrete equally to all shareholders but its risks do not: campaigning against a board cannot but jeopardise other corporate relationships. The swelling ranks of retail investors, drawn into equities in the 1990s by privatisations and demutualisations, are even less inclined, and less able, to agitate. Regimes of continuous disclosure have increased quantity of available data about companies, but the suspicion lingers that this has come at expense of quality – wealth of information, the economist Herbert Simon once observed, usually leads to poverty of attention.

The inconclusive results of the first wave of shareholder activism point up its other great weakness. It tends to intensify when economic times are tough, as lacklustre profits become to some degree unavoidable, and lose focus and impetus at the instant the market turns. CEOs survived their brush with bellicose shareholders in the mid-1990s for the same reason that the shortcomings of stock options were overlooked: because the market abruptly went gangbusters.

OVERSHOOT FIRST, ASK QUESTIONS LATER

Why do people invest? The traditional explanation is greed, fear and greed – but never underestimate fear. Alexander Pope rationalised purchasing shares at the South Sea Bubble's fullest inflation by referring to the fear of not doing so: "'tis ignominious (in this Age of Hope and Golden Mountains) not to Venture". Even once decisions are made, a streak of irrationality persists. In their delightful *Bulls, Bears and Dr Freud*, San Francisco stockbroker Albert Haas and Stanford psychiatrist Don Jackson concluded that investment was as much personality- as purse-driven. An investor gravitated to stocks that "it makes him feel good to own", they decided: "Just as a flag is only a symbol for a country, so a stock merely represents shares of ownership in a company. Yet there are stock worshippers as well as flag worshippers."

Both impulses were evident during the 1990s. When analysts were prophesying a virtually indefinite boom staked by baby boomer billions, not to venture seemed ignominious indeed. And frankly, a good feeling was all one could have about most internet stocks born after Netscape's initial public offering in August 1995, with their non-existent profits and semi-coherent strategies. Apologists for booms always stress that theirs is different – and they are partly right, for each reflects the character of its age. While the business heroes of the 1980s had positioned themselves as outside the establishment, the avatars of the 1990s boasted of building a new one, based on a kind of anti-corporate corporatism. Cuddly was in: when Netscape's Marc Andreessen appeared on *Time's* cover in February 1996, his bare feet told us he wasn't just another CEO. Cosmetic was cool: Amazon's Jeff Bezos rented a garage in Bellevue simply to say that his company had been founded there, joining the lineage established by the founders of Apple and Hewlett-Packard. Garages, indeed, were integral to e-conography. From punk rock's original rehearsal studios were to be heard the strains of punk business. "Face it," lectured fashionable management guru Gary Hamel, "out there in some garage an entrepreneur is forging a bullet with your company's name on it. You've got one option: you have to shoot first."

The dotcom entrepreneurs' anti-corporate bravado, however, also obscured some breathtaking naiveté. In his memoir *boo hoo*, the erstwhile CEO of fashion e-tailer boo.com, Ernst Malmsten, expresses high-minded horror at budgetary targets: "Being an entrepreneur was not about making money; it was about making dreams come true." But this, it emerges, is because he is more concerned with designing a corporate cocktail than with trivialities like whether his technology platform works, let alone archaisms like determining demand: "Market research? That was something Colgate did before it launched a new toothpaste. The internet was something you had to feel in your fingertips." Even when boo burns $us180 million and is forced to come up with a rescue plan, Malmsten's biddable hipsters are fashion victims:

> "Let's call it Dolphin," Jay said.
> "Why?"
> "Because dolphins are intelligent. They're also friendly and if this is the plan that's going to save us, we need to name it after a friendly fish."
> "Dolphins are mammals," I pointed out.

In the end, big-company CEOs would outdo almost everyone. Better a boss with stock options warmed by the general combustion than some geek feeding the flames. Silicon Valley even proved a useful ally when the Financial Accounting Standards Board proposed charging the cost of stock options against profits in 1989 and 1993. "If stock options aren't a form of compensation, what are they?" asked Warren Buffett. "If compensation isn't an expense, what is it? And, if expenses shouldn't go into the calculation of earnings, where should they go?" But experts could always be found to emphasise the dependence of the New Economy on equity-based remuneration, with a reverent glance at Bill Gates' self-propagating fortune. "No one points the finger at Bill Gates for being too rich," groused Al Dunlap when his Scott Paper millions were criticised.

ImClone's Sam Waksal snorted: "Has anybody ever said to Bill Gates: 'Gee you've made a lot of money on the company you built – that's really terrible!'?" Capitol Hill provided further gratuitous encouragement with a well-intentioned but ill-considered 1994 law capping the deductibility of executive salaries at $us1 million. This only resulted in bigger ransoms: by 2000, fully fourth-fifths of CEO compensation in the US came in the form of stock and bonuses.

As well as making them rich, the 1990s helped make CEOs famous. Economic historian Robert Shiller notes that a credulous media is a precondition of all bull markets: "The history of the speculative bubble begins roughly with the advent of newspapers." Nineteen CEOs made *Fortune*'s cover in 1999, breaking records of fifteen established in 1987 and 1993 (compared to only eight in the entire 1970s). *Time* garlanded two as Men of the Year: Intel's Andy Grove in 1997, Amazon's Bezos in 1999. New business media like CNNfn, CNBC and Bloomberg Television seemingly willed the market higher on behalf of the eager new investment generation. And it was the essence of the boom that it thrust individuals into the limelight, not only because the modern cult of celebrity demanded superstars, but because personalising a company, concept or creation was often the only way to nail it down. Numbers were drained of meaning. In 1998, AOL rose 593 per cent, Yahoo 584 per cent, Amazon 970 per cent. All were still burning money. But what were backward-looking accounts in a forward-looking world? One might as well judge a painting by the number of brushstrokes. No wonder a Burson-Marsteller survey found that 95 per cent of respondents were influenced in stock selection by the CEO's profile and reputation. At what else could one look?

The 1990s boom was somewhat unusual in that, after a time, its derangement was widely acknowledged. Dotcoms were known to be worth fractions of their stated values, telcos to have over-spent on acquisitions, and the meretricious accounts of the likes of Enron regarded with suspicion. Investors could be observed exchanging knowing nods and sly confidences: "How crazy is this market?" But a maxim of speculation is that just because it's fake doesn't mean it's not real. Investors always buy after they believe stocks over-valued, then sell after they believe them undervalued; as a banker admits in Charles Mackay's **1841** classic, *Extraordinary Popular Delusions and the Madness of Crowds*, "When the rest of the world is mad, we must imitate them in some measure." The Bigger Fool Syndrome prevails: the soothing sense that however foolish your purchase, a Bigger Fool will buy you out. In **1999**, Amazon shares were being held for an average seven days, compared to seven months for Microsoft and twenty-six months for Coca-Cola. Even stranger is that those skittish punters with their casino mentality and *sauve qui peut* ethos behaved with no less wisdom, and possibly more, than larger investors. After all, among the biggest of the Bigger Fools were big corporates.

LET'S UNMAKE A DEAL

Some deals define generations. KKR's $us26.4 billion buy-out of RJR Nabisco in February 1989 had climaxed what *Time* called "The Game of Greed"; AOL's capture of *Time's* owner, Time Warner, in January 2000 likewise culminated what we might call "Zeal for the Deal". History's biggest merger was a ponderous push-me-pull-you: AOL, with sales of $us5.2 billion and 12,000 employees, was capitalised at $us163.2 billion; Time Warner, with sales of $us26.6 billion and 67,000 employees, was valued at $us83.5 billion. But the excitement at a collaboration between the dishy New Economy and the dowdy Old was irresistible.

The amalgamania of the time was already unprecedented. Worldwide mergers, worth $us2.4 trillion in 1998 and $us3.4 trillion in 1999, had created compounds once unthinkable, like ExxonMobil, BP Amoco, J. P. Morgan Chase, Pfizer Warner Lambert and DaimlerChrysler. The majority of takeovers in the second half of the 1990s were agreed rather than hostile, funded by equity rather than debt, within industries rather than without, and were usually founded on some commercial rationale: excess capacity (cars), static or diminishing markets (aerospace and defence contracting), falling commodity prices (oil and minerals), rising costs of new technology (telcos and banks) and research (pharmaceuticals).

Harsher light, however, revealed more disturbing traits. While the 1980s market for corporate control had usually entailed seeking undervalued assets, that of the 1990s often involved acquirers exploiting their own momentary over-valuation, using their inflated stock as collateral. AOL Time Warner has proved to be an egregious example: three years after combining, it was worth a quarter of its peak valuation of $us260 billion.

Many mergers were also based not on overpowering advantages in alliance but on a kind of *torschlusspanik*: the fear of being excluded. The

UBS/Swiss Bank and Citibank/Travelers mergers in March/April 1998, for example, inspired scores of imitators, with very mixed results. Sometimes, one begat the other. When AMP demutualised in June 1998, inexperienced investors valued it at as high as $35 a share – an over-generous mispricing that CEO George Trumbull sought to exploit by having AMP bid for rival insurer GIO. The bid sent a tremor through the insurance industry and, having earlier considered a bid for GIO himself, Ray Williams at HIH now expedited plans to acquire another insurer; FAI, it turned out, was in difficulties, and its boss Rodney Adler a willing, even alacritous, seller. "The list of potential takeovers was shrinking," says HIH's chronicler Mark Westfield, "and Williams didn't want to miss out." Both deals were disasters. Over-eager, under-prepared, AMP and HIH rushed into acquiring targets riddled with hidden losses and underestimated risks: HIH will not recover; AMP's survival as an independent enterprise is now in the balance, for GIO was the first in a string of acquisitions made primarily because it had the resources to make them.

Although a greedy and parasitic intermediation industry has evolved to enable mergers and acquisitions, the buying of corporate assets is always the easy part. Nobody has developed a template for what follows a merger. One of big business's dirty secrets is that few combinations fulfil expectations, even remotely. Dozens of studies have concluded that companies founded on mergers under-perform sector peers, here as elsewhere: the most thorough Australian analysis, by Tim Brailsford and Stephen Knights, revealed that bidding companies generally suffered increased costs and narrowed margins after takeovers, while headcounts proved stubbornly resistant to reduction. Every company embarking on a merger hopes to form part of the successful minority rather than the unsuccessful majority, yet somehow a shadow usually falls between the idea and the reality. As the archetypal 1980s predator Sir James Goldsmith acknowledged, "You cannot buy a company merely by buying its shares."

Broad reasons are usually not far to seek. Mergers entail upheaval in existing operations, usually imperceptible to the CEOs hatching them, the boards approving them and the investment bankers cheering them on. Delicate corporate structures are shivered to fragments. Managements accustomed to competing are told to co-operate. Workforces are combined with the expectation that many will go. When service standards suffer, competitors target dissatisfied customers, refractory suppliers and talented staff. Intra-industry combinations run the gauntlet of anti-trust legislation. Cross-border mergers are befogged by cultural misunderstanding. Such factors are always underestimated. "People ultimately learn to work together," said John Reed airily after Citibank, of which he was the CEO and cynosure, merged with Travelers. "They may not like it. They may complain a lot. But in five years time they'll be surprised at how well they've learned to get on." After nine months, he'd lost his confidence: "I'm trying hard to understand how to make this work. I will tell you that it's not simple, it's not easy, and it's not necessarily clear to me that it will be successful." The following month, he lost his job. In a structural sense, bigger is always harder — thus C. Northcote Parkinson's famous maxim that "growth brings complexity, and complexity decay". In a financial sense, bigger is also more expensive — while everyone hopes for a bargain, sellers set their price knowing that takeovers involve concentration on the chase rather than its object. However powerful and impressive the appearance of a united group, furthermore, it remains beholden to the business cycle and to market conditions. With its expansion in the UK, for example, AMP broadened and deepened its exposure to an equities boom about to peak and to an investment product strategy replete with risk. Size and scale conferred no market power; like a windjammer with all its canvas aloft in a hurricane, AMP finished its takeover spree more rather than less vulnerable to the forces it faced.

Given this ruinous record, why would any CEO voluntarily initiate a takeover? Two reasons usually suggest themselves. First, there's boredom. Takeovers are exciting and glamorous: it's more satisfying to spend billions on an acquisition than time on improving stock turn and reducing inventory. And then, there's vanity. Takeovers attract attention and kudos: a droll 1995 study by Columbia University's Matthew Hayward and Donald Hambrick confirmed statistically a long-suspected link between the premiums paid for target companies and the self-aggrandisement of CEOs, measured by salary and media exposure. If these reasons seem frivolous, they steer us towards a troubling third: that it's easy. The urge to merge often reflects pressure in a company's core business, the fixing of which would otherwise involve both detailed understanding of its operations and unpleasant choices. Although it's a short-term solution to a long-term problem, and generally hints at a poverty rather than a wealth of executive imagination, it's usually much simpler to acquire.

Everyone's happy when a merger is consummated. For the acquired, it's a big payday. Gilded ripcords release voluminous golden parachutes, such as the $33 million one on which Colonial's Chris Cuffe recently floated free from Commonwealth Bank. For the acquirer, big paydays impend. Like the generals of a junta pinning medals on one another, everyone rewards themselves with a pay rise and a hearty helping of options to reflect the larger group. After the analysts' approbation, of course, comes some hard graft: combining wary workforces, the search for savings, the elimination of duplications, the curbing of rivalries. But by the time cracks appear, shrewd dealmakers will already have departed. Cynics might suspect CEOs of steering companies toward acquisitions because they know that the credit for the compelling conception will be theirs, but the blame for the resultant write-downs and write-offs will not.

An excessively cynical formulation? One certainly hopes so. Yet such has been the cycle the market is geared to rewarding. Not so much conscious sabotage – although as Stanford's James Collins has observed, "What better testament to your personal greatness than that the place falls apart after you leave?" – as the privileging of short-term activity over long-term continuity. Because the value of options is enhanced by fluctuations in the value of the underlying security, the incentive is to grander designs, greater gambles. *Business* 2.0 recently published research by Stephen Bryan at Wake Forest University suggesting that companies with high concentrations of stock options tended to have more volatile prices. "In other words, if you're an executive with lots of stock options," said columnist Thomas Stewart, "it's in your interest to make decisions that increase risk and hence increase the amount by which a stock's value jumps around. That incentive is strengthened because you're playing with someone else's money. Since the option costs you nothing, you're more likely to play fast and loose than you would if the money were your own and hard-earned."

We have strayed a long way from the original idea that rewarding executives with stock would strengthen their sympathy with shareholders. On the contrary: because what gratifies investors in the short-term is not always in a company's interests long-term, it can provoke as many bad business calls as good. But there's more: as at Enron, sundry telcos and dotcoms, it may encourage dishonesty. Fully valued stock price: good. Over-valued stock price: better. Absurdly inflated share price based on sham accounts: best – at least if you're a seller.

What we'll politely call the inexactitude of financial statements has been an aspect of recent corporate capers that many have found baffling. Accountants are meant to be vigilant, diligent and dull. Accounts themselves, however, have always been infinitely flexible. Business lore is strewn with variations on the immortal exchange between Ford's Arjay Miller and his chief accountant Charles Martindale. Asked what profits would be next month, Martindale replied, "What do you want them to be? I can make them anything you want."

Inducements to creative accounting, of course, usually flow the other way, from chief to underling. And during the 1990s such propositions were usually heeded, because the underling already owed the chief a good deal. A 1999 CFO poll found that 39 per cent of CEOs had fired their last chief financial officer, and three-quarters had personally hired the latest incumbent, mostly in the last three years. These CFOs, moreover, were not the beancounters of yore. A Spencer Stuart survey of *Fortune*

500 companies two years ago found that only a fifth of CFOs were certi-fied practising accountants. Quizzed about Enron's practices at the February 2002 congressional hearings following its collapse, its phari-saical CEO Jeffrey Skilling protested, "I am not an accountant." And neither was his CFO Andrew Fastow, nor his deputy Michael Kopper, nor treasurer Jeff McMahon. Nor was WorldCom's CFO Scott Sullivan, nor Global Crossing's CFO Dan Cohrs: like Skilling, they had either MBAs or possessed some other non-accounting qualification. No wonder they led the trend of designing profits to fit forecasts rather than vice versa.

Earnings "smoothing" is common enough. Welch's GE was so adept – timing asset sales, for instance, to offset re-structuring charges and write-downs – that it missed quarterly earnings forecasts only twice during his reign. Yet what became striking elsewhere was how eagerly the manipu-lation of financial accounts was abetted by like-minded auditors. Arthur Andersen's chief luminary in the mid-1990s, Steve Samek, would give inspirational speeches accompanied by a violinist, encouraging auditors to think of themselves as "maestros"; "fiddlers" might have been more apt. A core principle of conservative accounting, for example, is that decreases in an asset's value should be recognised at once, and increases only on sale. But, as with most bull cycles, the last incited so-called "mark-to-market" practices: immediate recognition of increases in the value of investments, usually with some effort to book in the growth as revenue even where the profit was not crystallised. Likewise, secret-ing some lumpy assets and their lumpier debts in special-purpose entities off the balance sheet appeared perfectly harmless, and treating infra-structure and marketing expenditures as investments to be written off over a number of years instead of charging them against earnings seemed only sensible. Especially when, if you wouldn't, someone else would, and dissent could be expensive. Having cultivated management consulting operations more lucrative than their accounting functions, the "Big Five" auditors were at the time so vulnerable to having their arms twisted that they usually did it themselves.

Respectable arguments exist for flexibility in accounting – not all businesses are the same. But when everyone indulges in it to greater or lesser degrees, exaggeration tends to become the norm: it is estimated that, at the height of the last boom, profits at the top 500 American companies were overstated by as much as 20 per cent. Regulators strained to keep pace. In 1981, American companies reported only three earnings restatements; between 1998 and 2000, they conceded 440. But the serious malefactors did themselves in long before they were caught.

The most surprising aspect of the creed of shareholder value is not that it encourages dishonesty, but that it seems to encourage little else. Empirical evidence that equity-based compensation makes more conscientious bosses, rather than merely rich ones, has proved stubbornly elusive. Studies at Harvard and Wharton in the late 1990s found that compensation of both executives and directors was not predictive of corporate performance. James Collins reached similar conclusions in the studies that composed his best-selling *Built to Last* (1994) and *Good to Great* (2001): "The idea that the structure of executive compensation is a key driver in corporate performance is simply not supported by the data." As for Australia, CEO salary inflation cannot be said to have enhanced profitability: a recent IBISWorld survey revealed that after-tax returns on equity at the country's top 1000 businesses had almost halved in fifteen years.

This, of course, challenges all the pieties. If holding shares doesn't make feckless managers behave like responsible owners, what will? It's arguable, though, that the CEOs retrofitted as owners during the 1990s failed not because they didn't act as shareholders, but because they did. Equities culture since the beginning of the bull market increasingly came to stress trading and turnover; the dotcom stampede involved the minting of millions in minutes. Perhaps bosses merely decided that when in Babylon, they should do as the Babylonians. If their corporation had no purpose other than to create shareholder value, so what if, at the end of the day, it did not exist? And no wonder, under this philosophy, that it often ceased to.

Given that this situation is unlikely to change, should we abandon the shareholder value paradigm? Not necessarily. Bear in mind that recent trends involved a very particular variant of the creed, accented to capital growth. Were we to think of shareholder wealth in terms of dividends distributed, the CEOs who have bankrolled their ambitions by arrogating excess profits to themselves over the last decade have served investors appallingly. How much better off would shareholders at AT & T, Allianz and BHP have been if their companies had disgorged the cash they were about to fritter away on TCI/MediaOne, Dresdner Bank and Magma Copper respectively? What it would be helpful to do, however, is grasp that maximising short-term profits has costs. A degree of waste, of duplication, of excess expense, may be the difference between an inviting workplace and a demoralised one; stored in the way creatures accumulate fat and ships carry ballast, it provides a buffer against the unforeseen. Anecdotally, it's probably better to be a little inefficient than too astringent. At Britain's retail flagship Marks & Spencers, for example, the cost consciousness of old boss Simon Marks ("Good goods will sell arse upwards," he once said) and the £1 billion profit obsession of new boss Richard Greenbury wrought a heavy toll. Though floor space was expanded by almost a third between 1991 and 1998, it kept such a tight lid on headcount that finding assistance became nigh impossible; the retailer's old aversion to fitting rooms and toilets, and to stocking baby or XL clothes, also smacked increasingly of high-handedness. The outcome was inevitable: a sudden, alarming collapse in sales five years ago that almost cost the chain its independence.

The difference between efficiency and effectiveness, though, is best illustrated by the meagre dividend of downsizing in the late 1980s and early 1990s. Most big job hackers became repeat offenders: one celebrated survey found that two-thirds of big payroll shrinkers had to do it a second and even a third time. Strangely, it is still considered a tribute to refer to a CEO as "a cost fanatic". But a fanatic, as George Santayana remarked, is one who redoubles his efforts when he has forgotten his aims. Sharp increases in returns on shareholders' funds can be a warning: someone is stinting where they haven't been; someone is running more risks than they were.

The view of the corporation as a means to the creation of shareholder value should be seen as comparable to that much-despised fantasy figure Rational Economic Man: a useful simplification, but a silly assumption. It's helpful for CEOs to think of serving shareholders; what's destructive is sacralising the shareholders' position and doing everything legal, less legal and downright dubious in order to enrich them. This isn't because the service of shareholders encourages the pauperising of what are now popularly known as "stakeholders" — that weird word, with its quaint echo of Dracula's nemesis, Dr Van Helsing. It's simply bad commercial sense. A company is no more its share price than a book is its title. Short-term measures to pump up a price simply benefit a few lucky sellers at the expense of the rest. Warren Buffett's words, as ever, are wisest: "We do not wish to maximise the price at which Berkshire Hathaway shares trade ... We wish for them to trade in a narrow range centred at their intrinsic value." We are in danger of confusing means and ends: companies do not exist to make profits; they make profits in order to exist. To say otherwise, Peter Drucker has observed, is to substitute legal fiction for social reality: "The corporation is permanent, the share-holder is transitory. It might even be said without exaggeration that the corporation is really socially and politically *a priori* whereas the share-holders' position is derivative and exists only in the contemplation of law."

Charles Handy dismisses as myth "that it is the shareholders who run the business and that it is for them that we all work". He champions "existential" corporations: "What, then, is a company for in this new, more blended, world? The only real answer, I suggest, is 'for itself'." This pushes us too far in the direction of unaccountability and opacity: democracy's shortcomings do not justify autocracy. But sound reasons exist for reducing shareholders to the ranks, as it were. Legally, share-holders are the lowest-ranked and least secure creditor. And despite incitements to activism, most fund managers still behave more like passive financiers than actual owners. So how have their interests come to precede all others? Marjorie Kelly has argued that shareholders, like feudal lords, contribute nothing yet expect the lion's share of wealth:

> The productive risk in building businesses is borne by entrepreneurs and their initial venture investors, who do contribute real investing dollars, to create real wealth. Those who buy stock at sixth- or seventh-hand, or one-thousandth hand, also take a risk — but it is a risk speculators take among themselves, trying to outwit one another, like gamblers.

The irreverent might wonder whether responsible CEOs should align their interests with such reprobates at all.

CULTURE VULTURES

The stock market wasn't the only market CEOs tended during the last decade; turnover in another security, thinly traded but eye-catching, was followed with special avidity: themselves. At one time, executives rose to leadership on seniority and technical skill. Decades of business-school education and the development of management accounting systems changed all that. When all candidates for a job have similar backgrounds and access to similar information, other factors distinguish them. Rosabeth Moss Kanter famously concluded that advancement in big business boiled down to five factors: appearance, personality, aggressiveness, executive stature and promotability. "The interesting thing about these five essential ingredients", she remarked, "is that they don't include professional competence." She conjectured that above a certain hierarchical level, competence was assumed – the emphasis fell instead on relations with peers and subordinates.

This had two implications. It became possible to reach the top of a corporation, to quote Henry Mintzberg, "without ever getting your hands on the clay of industrial experience". The days when retail magnate J. C. Penney taught his own staff to wrap goods, and Walt Disney wandered Disneyland picking up garbage, were past. It also became an option to recruit at senior level from outside your company, your industry, even your country: if a corporation was a corporation, and personal chemistry the key to success, the bosses to employ were outsiders with existing track records rather than insiders who might develop them. Thus, the rise of the "brand-name CEO". Lee Iacocca had merely moved from one leading industry participant to another; the brand-name CEO, like Lou Gerstner, superman of American Express, RJR Nabisco and IBM, leapt tall industries in a single bound.

The demand for brand-name CEOs was fostered by the bull market: this both allowed big compensation packages larded with options and encouraged the idea that merely incremental growth was insufficient to guarantee survival. The times, according to the quotable Gary Hamel, called not for "accountants" and "administrators", with their "exaggerated confidence in great execution", but for "visionaries". No matter that these visionaries might be unfamiliar with the industries to which they were recruited. On the contrary – newcomers were needed who would not be the captives of past practices. As Harvard's Rakesh Khurana has pointed out, the concept of the brand-name CEO is an explicit denigration of specialist operational know-how: the premium attaches to "the ability to inspire and motivate employees and instil confidence in analysts and investors", while "merely managerial tasks are discounted as pedestrian and boring, or simply ignored as irrelevant".

With its smaller talent pool and range of blue chip jobs, Australia has been fertile field for brand-name CEOs, either international or inter-industry. Coles Myer has had three consecutive appointments from outside its own ranks: Peter Bartels (Fosters), Dennis Eck (American Stores) and John Fletcher (Brambles). Likewise AMP: George Trumbull (Cigna), Paul Batchelor (Colonial) and Andrew Mohl (at the life office six years, but hired from ANZ). Telstra went first for American telecommunications veteran Frank Blount (AT & T), then a professional executive, Ziggy Switkowski (Kodak and Optus); Westpac followed suit with an American banker, Bob Joss (Wells Fargo), then a public servant, David Morgan (Department of Treasury). Oil executives came to run banks and fund managers, investment bankers to run construction, media and manu-facturing companies, management consultants to run everything. The phenomenon, too, has been sufficiently long-lived to attract apologists and apostates. James Strong, having run airlines, a law firm and a brewery, believes unsurprisingly that, "The fundamental skills that anyone's looking for in a CEO are very widely applicable." On the basis of thirty-five years at the construction group Leighton, sixteen as CEO, Wal King demurs: "I have a terrific love for this industry and the people and the camaraderie … So I don't agree with the concept that a professional manager can man-age any industry that comes along."

That bosses believe in an external CEO market isn't surprising. Hitherto, they'd followed in predictable ruts, with only a wealthy retirement to look forward to; how much cheekier to flirt with head-hunters and play hard-to-get with the boards of rival companies. Yet a moment's reflection offers myriad objections. A company that decides to seek an outside CEO indicts itself, effectively conceding not only inadequate succession planning but lack of management depth. And where this is not actually the case, incumbent executives could be forgiven for feeling slighted, if not thwarted in regard to their own ambitions. This is important: external appointments always assume that the conditions under which the new CEO previously operated can be exactly replicated, both in terms of the challenges faced and the executive talent and resources available to meet them. Book after turgid management book has extolled the virtues of "teams" – yet we still think of the CEO singly, a heroic Hercules on stable duty for Augeas.

Khurana observes that the circumstances of external CEO appointment are inescapably compromised. Boards know nothing of how their new man works; they rely instead on scuttlebutt, rumour, intuition and prophecy. Typically, remarks Warren Bennis, directors "go into a kind of collective trance, rhapsodising about 'leadership' and the need for it without ever taking even the first step to define what they mean by the term". The structure of the market in CEOs, meanwhile, with its reliance on intermediation and the need for confidentiality, makes overpayment almost inevitable. Directors aren't spending their own money: they're acting on behalf of shareholders who'll have no say in the terms of the deal. And because companies create an artificial scarcity of candidates by restricting the search to a small group in the interests of secrecy, they preclude any opportunity for rival, cheaper tenders. Derek Bok has observed that, for a CEO, "offering one's services for unusually low rates may signal some sort of weakness and thus repel clients rather than attract them". Paying a CEO more, likewise, is commonly construed as demonstrating a board's commitment to hiring the best.

There is also an acute irony in the undergirding assumption of the external CEO market, that the issues confronting every industry are generally the same, and that specialist knowledge can simply be picked up "on the job". For all the perceived need for "visionaries", CEOs appointed from outside the corporation are likelier to rely on cookie-cutter cost-cutting initiatives, on strategies proposed by the pre-existing executive team that they are ill-equipped to challenge, or on generic solutions and expensive acquisitions mooted by fee-driven management consultants and investment bankers. "Worldly wisdom", J. M. Keynes observed, "teaches that it is better for reputation to fail conventionally than to succeed unconventionally."

The rise of the brand-name CEO, then, is management's ultimate triumph. The premium lies not in the creation of enterprise but in its administration, not in anything new but in delivering what's expected. Since corporate capital supplanted individual capital, the CEO has been strengthened at every step. For a long time, he was left alone to get on with his job. He cocooned himself in increasing creature comforts. He was invited to expand, diversify, invest, divest as he saw fit, as though the enterprise was his own. When he was finally criticised for having grown too distant from the legal owners of the enterprise, the shareholders, he was then enabled to take it over, through management buy-outs, or simply given large portions of it on hugely advantageous terms, through stock options. Finally, with the external CEO market, he was encouraged to treat the corporation as an opportunity off which to leverage, as a chance to build a reputation that might be parlayed into bigger personal rewards elsewhere. He has, then, never been richer, more powerful, more prominent … or less effective.

The fact is that the brand-name CEO has been an acute disappointment to apologists. The most successful, Lou Gerstner, has admitted that his most important decision involved not what he did but what he didn't: by not breaking IBM up, as many were advocating, he positioned it to offer holistic "solutions" rather than a product here and a service there.

Failures have been more conspicuous. In the US, GE's Gary Wendt and Target's Floyd Hall could not stave off disasters at Conseco and Kmart respectively; and how well have Coles Myer and AMP done with their hotshot recruits? Recent studies by Margarethe Wiersema and Jim Collins seem to vindicate the Buffettism that, "When a manager with a great reputation meets a company with a bad reputation, it is the company whose reputation stays intact." Wiersema "couldn't find a single measure" suggesting that changing CEOs improved the companies concerned, while Collins' analyses of enduring enterprises found a negative correlation between "larger-than-life celebrity leaders" and relative corporate performance.

It is strange, then, that there remains an unblinking faith in the power of one – encouraged by several million options. A popular feature of modern newspaper business sections and periodicals, for example, is the survey that purports to rank CEOs by their company's profitability, or analyses their remuneration as a proportion of capitalisation or share price/dividend growth. Such surveys are very nearly meaningless. Technically, they assume that all things are equal, despite the huge discrepancies between average returns on equity at different companies and in different industries. And their two abiding philosophical premises, that the CEO is sole author of a company's fortunes, and that annual net profit and/or share price faithfully express the exertions of the year for which the remuneration was paid, are not just patently false: they are pernicious myths.

Since Machiavelli, who observed that "some princes flourish one day and come to grief the next without appearing to have changed in character or in any other way", management thinkers have wondered how much control leaders actually have over an institution's affairs. The Florentine's musing still resonates today:

> I am not unaware that many have held and hold the opinion that events are controlled by fortune and by God in such a way that the prudence of men cannot modify them, indeed, that men have no influence whatsoever … Sometimes when thinking of this, I have inclined to the same opinion. Nonetheless, so as not to rule out free will, I believe that it is probably true that fortune is the arbiter

of half the things we do, leaving the other half or so to be controlled by ourselves.

No one would contend that CEOs make no difference at all. The CEO who is also a founder obviously wields immense influence, although holding on too hard too long invites disaster ("There is room for only one superstar at News International," Andrew Neil was told by a colleague after Rupert Murdoch ended his meteoric rise there). CEOs with the confidence of investors can also be a boon, for the responsibility to personify the company has grown weightier since "the market" acquired the status of the ultimate arbiter of corporate fortunes. In the dotcom boom, for example, a plausible CEO made up for a host of technical and financial shortcomings: Yahoo head-hunted a "proper" businessman, Motorola's Tim Koogle, to convince investors it had outgrown its youthful high spirits; Webvan's recruitment of Andersen Consulting's George Shaheen was considered a resounding vindication of e-commerce (which, alas, didn't prevent it going broke).

While the two are often mistaken, however, there is a world of difference between what we might call managing outward and managing inward. One is not a substitute for the other: preoccupation with the former fosters the delusion that crises are merely matters of perception that can be "managed". As Enron's share price slumped two years ago, Ken Lay lambasted not banks, rivals, investors or employees but his corporate communications department: "This is a public relations problem. Why can't you solve it?" Assessing a CEO's internal impact, meanwhile, is supremely awkward, because what you get in corporations is not what you see. Reputation and remuneration are assessed on a present profitability that is heavily based on historical decisions in which the recipient played no part. Even a business dependent on profit from short-term trading is the beneficiary of past efforts to build its name, capital base and credit rating. A resources company's CEO will owe much of his pay to the choices of his predecessors, to explore in certain places and to develop certain mines or fields. The boss of an information technology group or electrical goods manufacturer will benefit predominantly from brand names, patents and royalties long pre-dating him. Furthermore, projects and innovations initiated now may have no earnings or share price impact for many years – a fact that, as Charles Hampden-Turner and Fons Trompenaar have commented, fits rather less than well with market doctrines of individual responsibility:

> Giving top executives bonuses based on these [past] accumulations is like overpaying the person who waves his fingers over the player piano on which the tunes were programmed many years earlier. In practice, it is not possible to calculate what a current CEO owes to the corporation as a community, which has learned and gathered expertise over time, and what that community owes him for his contemporary activities. All we know for certain is that lavish bonuses and handshakes transfer money from the incorporated carrier of long-term commitments to the short-term extractor of personal benefits, and we must expect the long-term viewpoint to suffer as a consequence.
>
> For if, in fact, the top manager is receiving rewards owed to the work of his predecessors, but does not acknowledge this and accepts most or all of the credit for current results, why would he bother to think of those who come after him? Let them make bold contemporary decisions as he has to earn their keep! The doctrine of individual responsibility ties each manager to shortened contemporary time spans. Proximate results are laid at your door, but distant results at another.

A CEO's choices can undoubtedly ramify for generations. Geoffrey Blainey has argued persuasively that Sir Ian McLennan's faith in geologist Lewis Weeks' recommendation that BHP explore Bass Strait for hydrocarbons contributed more to the nation's welfare than any single decision of the Whitlam government. But McLennan could scarcely have been *paid* for his decision *at the time*. And a decision only begins an implementation process. Where Bass Strait was concerned, success hinged, *inter alia*, on a sweeping seismic survey, on answering exacting challenges in pipeline and platform design, and on finding in Exxon an unusually accommodating joint venture partner to bankroll most of the exploration. Even then the field's first rig struck not oil but gas, about which BHP executives knew little, entailing a plant none had foreseen and markets none had imagined. Investments today take an even longer route, running the gauntlet of investors, analysts, fund managers, ratings agencies and trade unions, not to mention securities, anti-trust, foreign investment and environmental regulators. Then they must make a buck.

It could be argued, therefore, that with the partial exception of those functioning on dynastic bases, modern industrial corporations are un-amenable to one-man control – and that it was *meant* to be so. Alfred Sloan perceived his pioneering GM structure as "running itself" – so as to avoid the caprices of lone charismatics like his predecessor Durant and rival Ford – and efforts to change this have altered the corporation in detail but not in substance. In practical terms, as we have noted, CEOs can know only a fraction about the various processes in train in their corporations, and understand in detail even less. As knowledge becomes more special-ised, Isaiah Berlin once noted, the fewer are those knowing enough to be wholly in charge:

> One of the paradoxical consequences is therefore the depen-dence of a large number of human beings upon a collection of ill-co-ordinated experts, each of whom sooner or later becomes oppressed and irritated by being unable to step out of his box and survey the relationship of his particular activity to the whole. The co-ordinators always did move in the dark, but now they are aware of it. And the more honest and intelligent ones are rightly fright-ened by the fact that their responsibility increases in direct ratio to their ignorance of an ever-expanding field.

The CEO's active involvement in implementation these days is probably more circumscribed than ever. Yet bizarrely, as BHP Billiton's Paul Anderson complained last year, they've never been credited with greater powers: "Everything is attributed to the CEO whether it's good or bad. It's: 'The CEO did this, the CEO did that.' But in the case of BHP Billiton, 5 0,0 0 0 people did something and the CEO just happened to be standing there while it all happened." Caught between sanguine subordinates and sceptical directors, CEOs will pore ever more intently over the figures funnelled to them – aware, of course, that these too are negotiable. Within reason, they will seek to satisfy themselves that developments are proceeding as planned. They may even be capable of averting big miscalculations. But, as Anthony Jay has suggested, the real signs of industrial entropy cannot fail to elude them:

> If you are running a giant corporation, you have plenty to do without worrying about who is minding the shop. Yet the corporation may be crumbling away beneath you, and your customers may find it out before you do. It will not be dramatic, with millions of dollars suddenly changing hands on the balance sheet; it will be myriads of tiny, imperceptible failures. The car key that jams in the lock after three days, the shop assistant who does not know what she has in stock, the service engineer who promises to call and doesn't, the sullen, unhelpful girl on the switchboard, the travelling salesman who is obviously going through the motions of selling, without any conviction – all these and hundreds like them will happen from time and time in any corporation, but if allowed to multiply they can build up almost insensibly until they are a talking point among customers and start the long slow slide down the hill. They are beyond the direct control of a top corporate executive.

We confront here some elemental questions: why do some corporations cohere while others tend towards chaos? Such ponderings are loosely grouped under the heading "corporate culture". In his report on HIH, which has frequent recourse to the phrase, Justice Owen defines "corporate culture" as "the charisma or personality – sometimes overt but often understated – that guides the decision-making at all levels of an organisation". A more succinct summary might be "the way people work when they think nobody is looking". In a bad culture, they're probably looting the stationery cabinet, forging expenses chits and downloading porn, like the miserable galley slaves in the Slough branch of Wernham Hogg on television's *The Office*; in a good culture, they may be checking a consignment, streamlining a process or consulting a customer about their needs, like the perky folk of Wal-Mart with their company songs and corny stunts. Most corporations feature a bit of both; informal homeostatic mechanisms counter one with another.

Culture is a phenomenon perceptible, as it were, only out of the corner of one's eye. It registers in routines and rituals, lore and legend. It springs sometimes from a guiding principle, such as Nordstrom's famous instruction to staff, "Use your good judgement in all situations." It is manifested in gestures, like the freedom HP and 3M allow for unsupervised research, acknowledging that innovation springs from curious tinkering as often as from concerted R & D; and like Merck's decision simply to give away the anti-river blindness drug Mectizan when no African government could afford it because failure to do so might have demoralised its scientists. It transcends group hugs and team-building tosh. Some companies thrive on a sense of lawlessness: the Apple ethos, Steve Jobs once rationalised, involved it being more fun to be a pirate than to join the navy. But culture is usually inculcated by a sense of shared values, common attributes and what organisational theorists call "fair process": open, apolitical decision-making that nurtures trust and creativity.

If this sounds like commonsense, that's because it is. Most writing about corporate culture is pretentious, as though the insight that people look to their jobs for more than money is somehow as significant as decrypting DNA. The title "Director of Human Resources" still sounds eerily Orwellian, suggesting a form of personal strip mining that leaves only human craters and human tailings. Pity, really. While its study involves wrestling with ambiguities and searching for behaviours that must by definition occur out of sight, culture matters. Just as social maladjustment is often rooted in familial dysfunction, so corporate failure usually correlates closely with cultural weakness. And where this used to be a matter of organisational rigidity and conformity preventing adaptation and innovation, dynamic fluidity and flexibility have turned out to pose their own perplexities

Consider Enron. Technically, it crumbled because it applied its model of trading wholesale electricity and natural gas to asset classes where it did not fit and where the company lacked expertise, while sneaking more and more debt into off-balance-sheet hidey-holes. But its crisis was brought on by a free-wheeling culture that assumed smart people thrown enough money could conjure markets out of nothing. Ken Lay dreamed of employing "a superstar in every key position"; Jeffrey Skilling exalted his "water walkers". They flourished in an echo chamber of approval from management consultants – whose industry, of course, is based on a comparable *amour propre*. Enron had what McKinsey called "the talent mind-set", that is, "a deep seated belief that having better talent at all levels is how you outperform your competitors". Its consultants raved: "Few companies will be able to achieve the excitement extravaganza that Enron has in its remarkable business transformation, but many could apply some of the principles." But the excitement, as described by journalist Mimi Swartz, proved too much of a good thing – if it was ever good to begin with:

> The company was forever re-organising, so no one ever really knew who they were working for or what, exactly, they were supposed to be doing. The company put ever younger and less experienced people in charge of business units. The company threw ungodly amounts of money at new business concepts ... and was enveloped in chaos.

There were six complete re-structurings at Enron in its last eighteen months. The GE-style rank-and-yank evaluation system, whereby its performance review committee annually proscribed the weakest 1 0 per cent of employees, was torturous:

> In the middle stood representatives at Enron's Human Resources Department, who, much like game show hostesses, advanced or demoted employees according to their rankings by moving placards with their names toward the front or back of the table ... In the PRC's earliest incarnations, committee members routinely grabbed a placard from the top of the table – "*There is no way in hell this guy is a water walker!*" – and shove the card of some hapless youth down the

end of the table with the rest of the losers … Once they were weeded out, managers had to choose between people who were cool and people who might be just marginally cooler … Committee members began running down employees they hardly knew just to save their own. Executives … sacrificed good people just to go home and get some sleep.

The result was a company that, especially in new businesses like bandwidth trading, was locked in mortal combat with itself:

The Houston traders kept threatening to sell the entire network, which would kill the business the Portland people had started. As revenge Portland started throwing away contracts to keep deals from moving forward. Or they would sign a contract and not tell anyone in Houston including the lawyers. That act of defiance would be followed by massive sackings in Portland, which would be followed by more sabotage.

Australia's outstanding recent case study is One.Tel, as ineptly run as it was incompetently led. The philosophy of CEO Jodee Rich, as described by journalist Paul Barry, was "a mixture of Deepak Chopra, est and New Age management theory". The words "desk" or "meeting" were prohibited. Its "Beliefs and Values" enjoined workers to "Take time to think" and "Lie on the grass". But as the company churned and burned thousands of customers, chaos reigned:

Finding the person responsible for doing a particular job could be a nightmare. The telephone list didn't tell you who did what and no one had offices, so new managers found themselves wandering down the rows of pods, asking for people by name. The lack of job titles made it easy for people to claim it was not their job to do what was needed.

Insiders told Barry that One.Tel was "run like a fish and chip shop", with "no structures, no accounting systems, no processes and no controls". The openness, too, was skin deep. "Why don't you focus on the positives?" Rich would say when managers pleaded for staff and resources. "What wins have you had today?" When One.Tel's billing system collapsed, no one dared tell him; when call centres overloaded, operators simply "dumped":

> An experienced dumper could get rid of 5 0 0 0 calls a day by answering the phone on mute, hitting the transfer button and pressing autodial, which brought the caller back into the One.Tel switchboard as a new call. The trick worked wonders with the figures. The system scored the dumping as 5 0 0 0 calls answered and 5 0 0 0 fresh calls received – so there was a huge increase in productivity and a corresponding fall in average wait times.

Culture, it could be argued, has seldom mattered more. Companies have never been larger, more complex, more dispersed, less supervised. Most of our work in a given day doesn't happen because someone told us to do it; it occurs because of unspoken understandings about our role, and trust in our commitment to a common cause. For all their forbidding facades, says Harlan Cleveland, corporations today have never been closer to uncentralised systems – a development with many entailments:

> No individual can be truly "in general charge" of anything interesting or important. That means everyone involved is partly in charge. How big a part each participant plays will much depend on how responsible he or she feels for the general outcome of the collective effort.

Where does this leave CEOs? The company's profit and price cannot be reliably ascribed to what they do on a daily basis. Their actual business decisions will stand or fall on how well they are implemented. They were once vital and visible presences in their corporations, but now, above the fray, preoccupied with the demands of investors, analysts and the media, they've never seemed more remote: so many faceless suits, tarting up their franchises with a few acquisitions, occasionally screwing down costs to keep shareholders sweet, and demanding unswerving loyalty even while they're being schmoozed by head-hunters, as their rewards depart ever farther from the mean. Far from preserving their corporation's cultures, they might even be endangering them.

Having looked at how CEO compensation grew so great, let us consider why it remains so. Money, of course, contains not only value but values. Critic Keith Jackson has observed, "However fulsome the lip service a society may pay to the professions which do not directly produce wealth – teaching, nursing, fighting fires – the salaries of those engaged in these jobs reveal what the society really considers valuable." Because we regard corporations as engines of wealth creation, and respect hierarchy and rank, we reward those at least nominally in charge. We retain, too, an irreducible belief in money's motivating properties. Even were we to accept that the CEO's role in a corporation is not decisive, there would remain an argument in favour of high levels of compensation. According to the "tournament theory" of executive remuneration delineated twenty years ago, companies pay their CEOs outsized salaries not to keep recipients happy but to cajole those vying to succeed them. "The CEO gets to enjoy the money," the theory's progenitor, Ed Lazear, explained. "But it's making everybody else work harder." Overall compensation costs would be lowered because competing subordinates effectively sacrificed some of their legitimate remuneration to provide the "pot".

Not surprisingly, "tournament theory" has proved enduringly popular among CEOs, fond of sport and competition as well as money. It even has some anecdotal correlatives: consider how the law and medicine, by sweating articled clerks and junior doctors, have traditionally used wage differentials as a stimulus. But how robust is "tournament theory"? When Graef Crystal tested the assumption that top managers at 200 American companies were accepting a discount on their market value for the sake of the stake, he found that the opposite was true: there was a strong statistical correlation between the pays of the CEO and of the second-highest executive, the second with the third, and so forth. "The pay of a CEO is not unlike a 4000-horsepower vacuum cleaner: it sucks up the pay of anyone else who gets close to the nozzle," he concluded. "We have to assume that giving the CEO an extra dollar of compensation has a multiplier effect; perhaps in the end that extra dollar will cost the shareholders

$40 or $50 when you consider the effect it has on sucking up the pay of executives on many different management levels." Which is the sort of finding that could surprise only an economist: commonsense tells you that the usual response to the sight of others getting ahead is raised, not lowered, expectations.

Commonsense tells you some other things too. Money is not only a motivator; it can also de-motivate. The exorbitant rewards of a boss they do not know, never see and barely understand hardly stirs a middle manager or worker to greater effort. The disruptive effect of big rewards was first systematically observed in the late 1930s by Joseph Scanlon, an accountant and union official at LaPointe Steel in Pennsylvania, who staved off bankruptcy with a pioneering experiment in compensation re-structuring: he noted that where bonuses were paid to a group of workers, that group was likelier to support and respect higher performers, but where bonuses were targeted to outstanding individuals, the result was enmity, disunity and sometimes outright sedition. One can only speculate on the corrosive impact of buoyant CEO salaries, especially in a period of profit stagnation, not to mention the trend to gross executive payouts on resignation, retirement and even retrenchment when all jobs are threatened. Some have criticised modern CEOs for being too obsessed with appearances; on the contrary, they may care too little. Ken Iverson of Nucor, the last American steelmaker worth the name, has pointed out what seems to have eluded so many others of his rank and generation:

> The people at the top of the corporate hierarchy grant themselves privilege after privilege, flaunt those privileges before the men and women who do the real work, then wonder why employees are unmoved by management's invocations to cut costs and boost profitability ... When I think of the millions of dollars spent by people at the top of the management hierarchy on efforts to motivate people who are continually put down by that hierarchy, I can only shake my head in wonder.

Big salaries, then, are not merely hard to justify; they may be com-promising the companies that pay them. And if CEOs are incapable of perceiving this, others will have to help them.

Corporate governance reform has tended to concentrate on boardrooms, as the coercive powers of not only shareholders but also regulators and auditors are necessarily limited. New codes of conduct for directors have recently been passed in the United States, Australia, Germany and Canada, while there have been four reviews of board behaviour in the City of London in the last decade.

In the ideal board meeting, none are silent and all are heard. The CEO provides initiative, the directors wisdom. But this ideal is elusive. Boards succumb easily to what psychologist Jerry Harvey calls the Abilene Paradox: groups agree to decisions that individual members inwardly acknowledge are silly because they know they can sidestep responsibility. At worst, a scene unfolds like the perfunctory board meetings in Anthony Trollope's *The Way We Live Now*, where the railway magnate *manqué* Augustus Melmotte quashes dissent in terms echoed by generations of executive egotists:

> Unanimity is everything in the direction of such an undertaking as this. With unanimity we can do – everything ... Without unanimity we can do – nothing. Unanimity should be printed everywhere about a Board-room ... If you and I quarrel in the Board-room, there is no knowing the amount of evil we may do to every individual shareholder in the Company.

Solutions abound to this tension between the quest for unanimity and the scope for disagreement. The US, UK and Australia tend to unitary boards but vary their compositions considerably: American companies have traditionally combined the roles of chairman and CEO and had more independent directors; British companies have separated the roles of chairman and CEO and had fewer independent directors; while Australian companies have leant one way or the other depending on their histories and ownership. In Germany, meanwhile, governance is split between the *vorstand* (management board) and *aufsichtsrat* (supervisory board, usually composed of various stakeholder representatives).

All these models are flawed. The American system has encouraged the collection of "trophy directors", kept largely for display; "wine 'em, dine 'em and screw 'em" was Henry Ford II's immortal advice. British non-executive directors, meanwhile, have tended to hold office out of custom, thanks to vestigial family connections. Jonathan Guinness recently revealed the extent of his family's incuriosity about the corporation bearing their name even as its CEO was involved in "dishonesty on a massive scale" during the takeover of Distillers. "It was always easiest to do nothing," he confessed, "so I kept my head down." Co-director Finn Guinness confided meekly in his brother, "We may not do much good but at least we don't do much harm." Australia has incorporated bits of both models, on occasions the worst of each.

Directors' responsibilities – and the cost of failing to fulfil them – have increased sharply in the last twenty years. Board members are now expected to serve on one or more internal governance bodies, such as committees concerned with the auditing of accounts, the remuneration of senior executives and the monitoring of regulatory compliance. A side effect, unfortunately, has been a diminution of the eligible candidates, especially in this country with its smaller corporate population. Bemoaning paltry fees and the threat of legal hostilities, the same current and retired CEOs turn up again and again, leavened by the occasional woman and academic. And because those most knowledgeable must often be disqualified because of perceived conflicts of interest, directors tend to be chosen not because of prior experience of the relevant industry but because of prior experience as directors. This has two entailments. First, their loyalty is owed primarily to the CEO and to their board peers rather than to the corporation or its shareholders. Second, they are acutely exposed to that gulf between the general knowledge at the top of organisations and the specialist knowledge within operations and finance. Katherine Schipper of the University of Chicago argued recently that a significant contributing factor to American corporate malfeasance was the "severe lack" of accounting expertise among directors, who relied instead on "gut instinct, oral tradition, managerial manipulation and casual conversation". One-eyed CEOs flourish easily in such kingdoms of the blind. They have the best view of the corporation's doings, fullest market intelligence, have been appointed by at least some of the directors, and have probably been involved at some level in the appointment of others. Directors remain dependent on the information management provides.

Discouragingly, no standard format exists for a successful board. In times of corporate puritanism, the cry is routinely raised for more independent directors. But while it is true that most scandals originate in management prodigalities, the independence of a board seems unrelated to its vigilance as a watchdog. Enron had a board that by some lights was close to ideal: only two executive directors and an audit committee chaired by a distinguished professor of accounting, Stanford's Robert Jaedicke. CEO Dennis Kozlowski was the only non-independent member of Tyco's board; an independent director ran board meetings, including sessions with executives from which Kozlowski was excluded. HIH, reports Justice Owen, "would have measured up reasonably well if its corporate governance system were checked off against most of the codes I have seen", while FAI "certainly would have done so". Close supervision, meanwhile, is a fine thing. Kerry Packer's legendary henchman Sam Chisholm has rightly remarked that, "There never was a company that went under because it had a board that was too strong." But a board should aspire to more than preventing a company's collapse: meddlesome directors scotching every initiative are as destructive as the dozy and neglectful.

Oddly enough, an obvious source of amply qualified directors, with undoubted loyalty and immense operational expertise, has been entirely overlooked. Given the modern obsession with selecting directors by their CVs, the recruitment of directors from among a company's former middle managers will sound heterodox to say the least. While the image of the CEO and top executive has been evolving for more than a century, the middle manager remains a Pooteresque caricature. Downsizing in the 1980s and 1990s annihilated hundreds of thousands; it remains the case that the quickest way for a CEO to obtain an ovation is to propose eliminating a layer of managers, as though dusting a mantelpiece or scraping off a coating of rust. Yet, as even Lou Gerstner acknowledges, bureaucrats hold companies together:

> The truth is that no large enterprise can work without bureaucracy. Bureaucrats ... provide co-ordination among disparate line organisations; establish and enforce corporate-wide strategies that allow the enterprise to avoid duplication, confusion and conflict; and provide highly specialised skills that cannot be duplicated because of cost or simply the shortage of available resources.

Under pressure, most CEOs will admit something similar: that middle managers are custodians of corporate culture and keepers of corporate memory. Actually, they're more. They understand processes, and the impact of policies. They deal daily with abrasive personalities, and have eyeballed competitors. There will be reasons, of course, why they have not risen to top management. They probably lacked ambition. They may have had limited horizons. Yet what a source of know-how for other directors to consult. And training operations personnel to evaluate board issues is surely no more difficult – and probably less – than schooling professional directors in operations. The likeliest objection – that middle managers are inherently suspicious of innovation and lack imagination – assumes that both are entirely negative qualities: more suspicion and less imagination would have saved billions at telcos and dotcoms, have thwarted a host of ill-considered acquisitions and re-directed innumerable ill-conceived austerity drives.

It will, of course, probably never happen. Directors are wedded to the recruitment of people like themselves. Which is a pity, for this seems all the more reason to promote from within and below. The archetypal middle manager has always put the corporation's interests before his or her own. They understand that their companies are more than "shareholder value" devices. They appreciate the long haul because they've been part of it. They also know how disaffecting it is for staff to look up at a CEO on a multi-million dollar salary. If we genuinely wish to curb over-mighty, over-rated, overpaid CEOs, there could be no better counterweight than those who've been none of these things while lending their enterprise unstinting service. But maybe, of course, we don't.

Dear Business Leader ...

Form letters abound in their variety, but the salutation on this one immediately lent it novelty. It arrived recently from *Harvard Business Review*, the journal seen in all the best executive briefcases.

Your career isn't just about money, is it?

That's for sure ...

I didn't think so. It's about something deeper.

Tell me more ...

Something so central to your core, to what makes you tick, that you can't imagine living without it.

I'm ready. Hit me with it.

It's about leadership. Having your say. Making things happen. Putting your stamp on the future.

Is that right? The point of this sycophancy was swiftly revealed. If I completed the enclosed form and committed my credit card to a monthly ravaging, I'd be privy to the latest wisdom on questions like "*The essential skill of managing oneself*" (which I rather liked, imagining issuing my own orders, refusing them, then firing myself). But was I up to the responsibility anyway?

To be a successful leader, you have to be smart, tough, determined and visionary.

Phew.

Sure, but stop there, and you're an also ran.

Eh? Did HBR mean that these qualities were not enough? Where did that leave those of us who were slow, meek, dilatory and introspective? All was revealed in the accompanying pamphlet, "*You and Harvard Business Review*". The combination, it seemed, was electric. The outcome was a CEO cut from the cloth of John Galt in *Atlas Shrugged*:

Leader. Strategist. Mentor. Architect. Builder. Co-ordinator. Champion.

LSMABCC had little to recommend it as a mnemonic, but as a formula it was both compelling and menacing, like the product of a religious ecstasy or a personality cult; one would not have been surprised to see it in a tract about David Koresh, or at a parade honouring Kim Jong Il. And therein, I suspected, a source of our present discontents. The making of the modern CEO has been a story of more: more power, more discretion, more ownership, more money, more demands, more expectations and, above all, more illusions. More, as so often, has brought less – and as Peter Drucker once observed, was always likely to: "No institution can possibly survive if it needs geniuses or supermen to manage it. It must be organised in such a way as to be able to get along under a leadership composed of average human beings." And if we think we need supermen to run our businesses, then the solution is not to seek supermen but to re-think business. The economist Paul Samuelson once described capitalism as "an effective but unlovable system with no mystique to protect it"; right now it should take some steps to protect itself.

Legislation and regulation have a part to play. A variety of proposals have been either accepted or aired, those in the US being of paramount significance, representing as they do the price of entry to the world's richest capital markets. The integrity of accounts must be restored as a priority: the expensing of stock options and restrictions on non-cash items in income statements cannot come quickly enough. Changes can be expected to the structure of compensation packages, not merely for the sake of fairness, but because of lacklustre stock markets: as Alfred Rappaport once said, CEOs always wish to be paid for absolute performance in bull cycles, relative performance in bear cycles. It will no longer be open to compensation committees simply to distribute fists full of options, let the invisible hand of the market work its magic, and claim that they are paying for "performance". On the contrary: we should probably expect a drift back to old-fashioned salaries, with a proportional increase in the uptightness of big investors. And it would not suprise if more companies resisted the windfall severance payments hitherto granted unblinkingly, as AMP did in March with Paul Batchelor. These gratuities have long been not only obscene but illogical, because, as we have seen, executive decisions so seldom bear fruit contemporaneously. Where a retirement benefit is decreed, it should be shaped by a company's long-term fortunes; where, otherwise, is the incentive to consider them? "A big award is justified only if it serves a useful purpose," commented the *Economist* recently, "such as persuading bosses to worry about what happens after they leave."

Other mooted changes to the law appear less likely to restrain CEOs, for the simple reason that legalities are not the same as ethics. Justice Owen muses in the HIH report, "From time to time as I listened to evidence about specific transactions or decisions, I found myself asking rhetorically: did anyone stand back and ask themselves the simple question – is this right?" The question can only have been rhetorical: CEOs and boards condone amongst themselves excesses that in other contexts they would probably condemn, as Stanford's Jeffrey Pfeffer recently observed:

> There are things that happen when you join a company that cause you to believe that the values in one's outside life aren't relevant anymore on the inside. You say: "The rules are different. Life is complex." So what has been going on recently really has more to do with an unsurpassed ability on the part of senior corporate leaders to justify anything.

Business in recent times has not, however, simply fallen among thieves. Corporate depredation has less impact on market cycles than market cycles on corporate depredation; thus John Kenneth Galbraith's famous theory of "the bezzle":

> At any given time, there exists an inventory of undiscovered embezzlement. This inventory – it should, perhaps, be called "the bezzle" – amounts at any moment to many millions of dollars … In good times people are relaxed, trusting and money is plentiful. But even though money is plentiful, there are always many people who need more … under these circumstances, the rate of embezzlement grows, the rate of discovery falls off, and "the bezzle" increases rapidly. In depression all this is reversed. Money is watched with a

narrow suspicious eye. The man who handles it is assumed to be dishonest until he proves himself otherwise.

Accumulating evidence of recent corporate corruption, then, has been received with rather too much relish, tending as it does to absolve everyone else. We forget that a lot of what CEOs extracted was in full view. We overlook how naively we bought the myth of their individual genius. We ignore our complicity in the "irrational exuberance" that made them rich. If we wish to avoid repeating this age's errors, we will need, above all, a more reasoned and realistic understanding of how businesses work, where value is added, where it is dissipated, what the CEO can do, what he assuredly cannot. We'll need to distinguish between activity and progress, between ostensible expansion and sustainable growth, between the quantity of a profit and its quality. And we'll have to abandon our fixation on the boss of the enterprise, a phenomenon whose only beneficiary has been a small and self-interested elite who would be just as effectual, just as motivated and wise and virtuous if they were paid a fraction of their current rewards.

Casting a big star may make a bad movie more watchable, but won't make it good. In the same way, the recruitment of a brand-name CEO at a mediocre corporation is likely only to make for a marginally more interesting version of failure. The modern industrial corporation was devised in order that commercial enterprise should outlive individuals and aggregate the talents of many: trying to turn it back into "the lengthened shadow of one man", to use Emerson's lovely line, was probably always foredoomed. Big companies are creatures of their cultures. What enables one to outperform another is far more mysterious than is generally assumed, and for the most part obscured from the outside world.

As for CEOs, we must seek from them a more modest appraisal of their abilities and powers. In some respects, it's very easy to be a CEO, precisely because the corporation has been designed to tick over, and structured so as not to depend on any individual genius. Ironically, this is not because it is an environment of impersonal control, but because it is a sum of human strivings. People adjust. People cope. People get by. A student of corporate collapses learns to marvel not only at the scale of human folly but at the power of human resilience. HIH underlines, yet again, how big businesses can cheat death for years, even decades, under management that would bankrupt a milk bar in a week. With this, however, comes the entailment that the corporation is very difficult to change; as its scale and complexity has increased, it has in fact grown less flexible and less responsive to control from the top. The most popular means of placing one's stamp on a company – mergers and aquisitions – are fraught with unseen perils and pitfalls. People resist. People ignore. Should it come to that, people quit. This represents one of our bosses' greatest challenges. CEOs should be worried about how they look, not merely to investors, to regulators and to media, but to their own employees. While scepticism is integral to a healthy corporate culture, cynicism is its greatest enemy – and for this the only remedies are honesty and humility.

SOURCES

"So a prudent man will always follow in the footsteps of great men and imitate those who have been outstanding. If his own prowess fails in comparison with theirs, at least it has an air of greatness about it." Thus Niccolo Machiavelli in *The Prince* — and on the desire for that air have publishers built a vast industry. Before World War II, Peter Drucker has recalled, "all the books on management did not fill a modest shelf." Then someone realised there was a buck in it — and today, perhaps no shelves in your local bookshop support so much dross. In an interview in March 1997, the veteran organisational scholar Richard Pascale recalled a recent meeting to discuss a book with a publishing company. All was well until the editor enquired, "But can you put your argument in one sentence?" When Pascale replied that, at a pinch, he might squeeze it into four, he was told to re-think the idea.

So be selective. Books quoted in this essay are the small tip of a vast and slow-moving glacier. Drucker's *Concept of the Corporation* (1946, The John Day Company) and *The Age of Discontinuity* (1969, William Heinemann) have resisted countless efforts to improve upon them. Henry Mintzberg's *The Nature of Managerial Work* (1973, Harper & Row) and *Mintzberg on Management* (1989, The Free Press) are personal favourites. Also quoted are: Albert, Michel, *Capitalisme contre Capitalisme* (1991, Seuil) (*Capitalism against Capitalism*, 1993, Whurr Publishers); Bennis, Warren and Nanus, Burt, *Leaders: The Strategies for Taking Charge* (1985, Harper & Row); Bok, Derek, *The Cost of Talent: How Executives and Professionals Are Paid and How It Affects America* (1993, Free Press); Burnham, James, *The Managerial Revolution: What Is Happening in the World* (1940, Indiana University Press); Cleveland, Harlan, *Nobody in Charge* (2002, Jossey-Bass); Collins, Jim and Porras, Jerry, *Built To Last* (1994, Random House); Collins, Jim, *Good to Great* (2001, Random House); Crystal, Graef, *In Search of Excess: The Overcompensation of American Executives* (1991, W. W. Norton); Garten, Jeffrey, *The Mind of the CEO* (2001, Penguin); Hamel, Gary, *Leading the Revolution* (2000, Harvard Business School Press); Hampden-Turner, Charles and Trompenaar, Fons, *The Seven Cultures of Capitalism* (1993, Doubleday); Handy, Charles, *The Empty Raincoat* (1994, Hutchinson); Harvey, Jerry, *The Abilene Paradox and Other Meditations on Management* (1996, Jossey-Bass); Huffington, Arianna, *Pigs at the Trough: How Political Corruption and Corporate Greed Are Destroying America* (2003, Crown); Jay, Antony, *Corporation Man* (1971, Pocket Books); Johnson, H. Thomas and Kaplan, Robert S., *Relevance Lost: The Rise and Fall of Management Accounting* (1987, Harvard Business School Press); Kanter, Rosabeth Moss, *Men* and *Women of the Corporation* (1 9 7 7, Basic Books); Kay, John, *Foundations of Corporate Success* (1 9 9 3, Oxford University Press); Kelly, Marjorie, *The Divine Right of Capital: Dethroning the Corporate Aristocracy* (2 0 0 1, Berrett-Koehler Publishers); Kennedy, Carol, *The Next Big Idea* (2 0 0 1, Random House); Khurana, Rakesh, *Searching for A Corporate Savior* (2 0 0 2, Princeton University Press); Lammiman, Jean and Syrett, Michel, *Entering Tiger Country: How Ideas Are Shaped in Organisations* (2 0 0 0, Roffey Park Management Institute); Lesieur, Frederick (ed.), *The Scanlon Plan: A Frontier in Labor–Management Cooperation* (1 9 5 8, MIT); Michaels, Ed, Handfield-Jones, Helen, and Axelrod, Beth, *The War for Talent* (2 0 0 1, Harvard Business School Press); Mills, C. Wright, *White Collar* (1 9 5 3, Oxford University Press); Pascale, Richard and Athos, Anthony, *The Art of Japanese Management* (1 9 8 1, Simon & Schuster); Riesman, David, *The Lonely Crowd: A Study of the Changing American Character* (1 9 5 0, Yale University Press); Sampson, Anthony, *Company Man: The Rise and Fall of Corporate Life* (1 9 9 5, HarperCollins); Whyte, William, *The Organization Man* (1 9 5 6, Simon & Schuster).

History

The outstanding scholar of the evolution of the modern industrial corporation is the Harvard economic historian Alfred Chandler, especially his *The Visible Hand: The Managerial Revolution in American Business* (1 9 7 7, Harvard University Press), *Pierre S. du Pont and the Making of the Modern Corporation* (1 9 7 1, Harper & Row), and *Scale and Scope: The Dynamics of Industrial Capitalism* (1 9 9 0, Harvard University Press). A complementary study of English malaise is Martin Wiener's *English Culture and the Decline of the Industrial Spirit 1850–1980* (1 9 8 1, Cambridge University Press). A range of journalistic and historical accounts of individual corporations and industries has also been drawn on: Anders, George, *Merchants of Debt: KKR and the Mortgaging of American Business* (1 9 9 2, Basic Books); Bevan, Judi, *The Rise and Fall of Marks & Spencers* (2 0 0 1, Profile); Brooks, John, *The Go-Go Years: The Drama and Crushing Finale of Wall Street's Bullish 1960s* (1 9 7 3, Weybright and Talley); Fukuyama, Francis, *Trust: The Social Virtues and the Creation of Prosperity* (Free Press, 1 9 9 5); Halberstam, David, *The Reckoning* (1 9 8 6, Avon); Katz, Donald, *The Big Store* (1 9 8 7, Viking); Kaplan, David, *The Silicon Boys* (1 9 9 9, Allen & Unwin); Lawson, Thomas, *Frenzied Finance* (1 9 0 5, Ridgway-Thayer); Levin, Doron, *Behind the Wheel at Chrysler* (1 9 9 5, Harcourt); McCraw, Thomas, *American Business 1920–2000* (2 0 0 0, Harlan Davidson); Sampson, Anthony, *The Sovereign State* (1 9 7 3, Hodder & Stoughton); Tarbell, Ida, *The History of the Standard Oil Company* (1 9 5 0, Peter Smith); Wilson, Mike, *The Difference between God and Larry Ellison* (1 9 9 7, William Morrow). For Australian experiences, I'm indebted to the company histories of Geoffrey Blainey, plus *The Politics of Big Business: A History* (December 1 9 7 6, Academy of the Social Sciences in Australia), while Justice Owen's *The Failure of HIH Insurance* (April 2 0 0 3, Commonwealth of Australia) was invaluable. Also consulted were: Barry, Paul, *Rich Kids* (2 0 0 2, Bantam); Gottliebsen, Robert, *10 Best and 10 Worst Decisions of Australian CEOs* (2 0 0 3, Viking); Hand, Graham, *Naked among Cannibals: What Really Happens inside Australian Banks* (2 0 0 1, Allen & Unwin); Sinclair, E. K., *The Spreading Tree: A History of APM and Amcor 1844–1989* (1 9 9 1, Allen & Unwin); Westfield, Mark, *HIH: The Inside Story of Australia's Biggest Corporate Collapse* (2 0 0 3, John Wiley & Sons).

Biographies

Because businessmen seem to write, produce or generate far more books than they read, this essay has been able to survey a broad spectrum of autobiographies and biographies. The following books by businessmen – or at least, as seems the modern fashion, bearing their names – are quoted herein: Dunlap, Al (with Bob Andelman), *Mean Business* (1 9 9 6, Times Business); Eisner, Michael (with Tony Schwartz), *Work in Progress* (1 9 9 8, Random House); Ford, Henry, *My Life and Work* (1 9 2 3, Doubleday); Gerstner, Louis, *Who Says Elephants Can't Dance?* (2 0 0 2, HarperBusiness); Guinness, Jonathan, *Requiem for a Family Business* (1 9 9 7, Macmillan); Iacocca, Lee (with William Novak), *Iacocca* (1 9 8 4, Bantam); Iverson, Ken, *Plain Talk* (1 9 9 7, John Wiley & Sons); McNamara, Robert, *The Essence of Security* (1 9 6 8, Harper & Row); Neil, Andrew, *Full Disclosure* (1 9 9 6, Macmillan); Rathenau, Walter, *In Days To Come* (1 9 2 1, Allen & Unwin); Rockefeller, John D., *Random Reminiscences of Men and Events* (1 9 0 9, Doubleday); Sloan, Alfred (with John McDonald), *My Years with General Motors* (1 9 6 3, Doubleday); Walton, Sam (with John Huey), *Made in America* (1 9 9 2, Doubleday); Watson, Thomas Jr., *Father, Son & Co.* (1 9 9 0, Bantam); Welch, Jack (with John Byrne), *Straight from the Gut* (2 0 0 1, Warner Books). Alphabetically by subject, the following biographies were consulted: Hagstrom, Robert, *The Warren Buffett Way* (1 9 9 4, John Wiley & Sons); Byrne, John, *Chainsaw: The Notorious Career of Al Dunlap in the Era of Profit-at-Any-Price* (1 9 9 9, HarperBusiness); Lacey, Robert, *Ford: The Men and the Machine* (1 9 8 6, Heinemann); Wright, J. Patrick, *On a Clear Day You Can See General Motors: John Z. De Lorean's Look inside the Automotive Giant* (1 9 7 9, Wright Enterprises); Wyden, Peter, *The Unknown Iacocca* (1 9 8 7, William Morrow); Blainey, Geoffrey, *The Steel Master* (1 9 7 1, Macmillan); Chernow, Ron, *Titan: The Life of John D. Rockefeller, Sr.* (1 9 9 8, Random House); Hessen, Robert, *Steel Titan: The Life of Charles M. Schwab* (1 9 7 5, Oxford University Press); Farber, David, *Sloan Rules* (2 0 0 2, University of

Chicago Press). Quotes from Gerry Harvey, James Strong, Wal King and Sam Chisholm are from *Executive Material* (2 0 0 2, Allen & Unwin), whose execrable cover obscures some interesting interviews by Richard Walsh.

Investment and Economics

The classic work on investment cycles is Charles Mackay's *Extraordinary Popular Delusions and the Madness of Crowds* (1 8 4 1, Richard Bentley). I have also quoted: Galbraith, John Kenneth, *The Great Crash of 1929* (1 9 6 1, Houghton Mifflin); Haas, Albert and Jackson, Don, *Bulls, Bears and Dr Freud: Why You Win or Lose on the Stock Market* (1 9 6 7, World Publishing); Shiller, Robert, *Irrational Exuberance* (2 0 0 0, Princeton University Press). The last outbreak of "irrational exuberance" is well documented from the outside by John Cassidy's *dot.con: The Greatest Story Ever Sold* (2 0 0 2, Penguin), and from the inside in Ernst Malmsten's *boo hoo: $135 million, 18 months ... dot.com story from concept to catastrophe* (2 0 0 1, Random House). Information on Enron is drawn from: Fusaro, Peter C. and Miller, Ross M., *What Went Wrong at Enron* (2 0 0 2, John Wiley & Sons); Schwartz, Mimi (with Sherron Watkins), *Power Failure: The Rise and Fall of Enron* (2 0 0 3, Aurum); and Malcolm Gladwell's fascinating article "The Talent Myth" (*New Yorker*, 2 7 July 2 0 0 2).

Views of economists on agency theory and the nature of managerial work are derived from: Berle, Adolf and Means, Gardiner, *The Modern Corporation and Private Property* (1 9 3 3, Macmillan); Olson, Mancur, *The Logic of Collective Actions: Public Goods and the Theory of Groups* (1 9 6 5, Harvard University Press); Williamson, Oliver, *The Nature of the Firm: Origins, Evolution and Development* (1 9 9 1, Oxford University Press). Mathew Hayward and Donald Hambrick proposed a connection between acquisition and ego in "Explaining the Premiums Paid for Large Acquisitions: Evidence of CEO Hubris", a contribution to *Administrative Quarterly* (no. 4 2, 1 9 9 7). The findings on Australian mergers by Tim Brailsford and Stephen Knights are from "Mergers and Takeovers: Should We Be Concerned?" in *How Big Business Performs* (1 9 9 9, Allen & Unwin). "Tournament theory" was outlined by Sherwin Rosen and Jeffrey Lazear in "Rank-Order Tournaments as Optimum Labor Contracts" in the *Journal of Political Economy* (October 1 9 8 1). Paul Samuelson's quote is from Robert Heilbroner's *The Worldly Philosophers* (2 0 0 0, Penguin).

Other Journal Articles

This essay draws heavily on reportage from *The Economist, Fortune, Forbes, Fast Company, Business 2.0, CFO, Eurobusiness, Business Review Weekly, Time* and *Newsweek*. Two excellent collections were extremely useful: *Best Business Crime Writing of the Year* (2 0 0 2, Anchor), ed. James Surowiecki, and *The New Gilded Age: New Yorker Looks at the New Culture of Affluence* (2 0 0 0, Random House), ed. David Remnick. Notwithstanding its quaint solicitation of subscriptions, *Harvard Business Review* from time to time lives up to its reputation as business's most influential magazine. Contributions cited or quoted by this essay are, in chronological order: "Selecting Strategies That Create Shareholder Value" (May–June 1 9 8 1) by Alfred Rappaport; "The Eclipse of the Public Corporation" (September–October 1 9 8 9) and "It's Not How Much You Pay, But How" (May–June 1 9 9 0) by Michael Jensen; "The Logic of Global Business: An Interview with ABB's Percy Barnevik" (March–April 1 9 9 1) by William Taylor; "The Promise of the Governed Corporation" by John Pound (March–April 1 9 9 5); "Bringing Silicon Valley Inside" by Gary Hamel (September–October 1 9 9 9); "Don't Hire the Wrong CEO" by Warren Bennis and James O'Toole (May–June 2 0 0 0); "What Makes Great Boards Great" by Jeffrey Sonnenfeld (September–October 2 0 0 2); "Holes at the Top: Why CEO Firings Backfire" by Margarethe Wiersema (November–December 2 0 0 2). Keith Jackson is quoted from "1 0 Money Notes" in *Granta* 49 (Winter 1 9 9 4). Jeff Madrick is quoted from "Welch's Juice" in the *New York Review of Books* (February 1 2, 2 0 0 2).

Literature, Film etc.

The following are quoted or referred to: Dickens, Charles, *Dombey & Son* (1 8 4 8); Heller, Joseph, *Something Happened* (1 9 7 4, Knopf); Levin, Ira, *The Stepford Wives* (1 9 7 2, Random House); Lodge, David, *Nice Work* (1 9 8 8, Secker & Warburg); O'Neill, Eugene, *A Moon for the Misbegotten* (1 9 5 2, Random House); Rand, Ayn, *Atlas Shrugged* (1 9 9 6, Signet); Trollope, Anthony, *The Way We Live Now* (1 8 7 5). Films cited are: *Executive Suite* (1 9 5 4, director: Robert Wise); *The Man in the Gray Flannel Suit* (1 9 5 6, director: Nunnally Johnson); *Other People's Money* (1 9 9 1, director: Norman Jewison); *Patterns* (1 9 5 6, director: Fielder Cook); *Silent Movie* (1 9 7 6, director: Mel Brooks); *Wall Street* (1 9 8 7, director: Oliver Stone). Isaiah Berlin's remark is from his *Conversations with Henry Brandon* (1 9 6 6, Deutsch).

George Seddon

"We'll all be rooned," said Hanrahan, in accents most forlorn. And so we will unless we listen and act. Tim Flannery's essay is a manifesto. We have heard some of it before, but not all, and here we have all thirty-nine articles passionately and clearly argued. Since I subscribe to all the principal tenets, I have little to offer other than marginal annotation – but it invites this at times, by the very force and speed of the argument.

The introductory three pages are nothing less than brilliant in linking so clearly the direct environmental costs of the Snowy scheme with the longer term environmental consequences of the ill-conceived population policy that was used at the time to justify it, while the two together have greatly reduced our capacity for a humanitarian response to the refugee problem we have helped create.

These three pages are what one might hope for in the editorials of the news-paper of a civilised and thoughtful nation in crisis. But we don't see them, and I am far from confident that the Australian public at large has any idea at all of, for example, how misconceived was the Snowy scheme. In Western Australia, letters still appear quite regularly in the local daily in support of Ernie Bridges' mad scheme to drought-proof the south-west by running a pipe-line down from the Kimberley. It has been shown very clearly more than once that the pumping costs alone would bankrupt the state, but that does not stop the *West Australian* from publishing letters of support. Should a responsible press behave thus? A similar story can be told for Queensland and western New South Wales: the spread of the cotton industry down the Darling almost to Bourke is on a par with rice-growing along the Murrumbidgee – flood irrigation with its huge evaporation loss on the driest continent on earth?

Sheep and Cats (with Fire to come)

If widespread environmental degradation is generally recognised, who are the chief villains, apart, of course, from us? Flannery passes sentence on sheep and

European pyrophobia, while cats get a remit. I am sure about the sheep. They have done immense damage in the pastoral rangelands, made worse by inadequate public and private policy. Only South Australia has been able to put sensible management policies in place. Sheep have eaten out the palatable species in huge areas of semi-arid Australia, and their jack-hammer hooves have pulverised the topsoil, leaving it to blow. One of our principal exports has been topsoil. All the hooved mammals have contributed to this, including feral goats and buffalo, but the sheep have been the worst. In a book coming out this year I put my view that "Waltzing Matilda" should be our national anthem – because the swagman killed and ate the jumbuck.

Flannery's assertion that cats are not especially destructive is well worth considering, and he is probably right. Dr John Walmsley, it seems, is a victim of woolly thinking, while Flannery has "good science" on his side – we have his word for it. The examples he adduces to show that cats do not cause extinction are very plausible, especially the case of the large islands, Kangaroo Island and Tasmania, which both have feral cats but have lost only the Dwarf Emu (Kangaroo Island) and the thylacine, neither from cat predation. Removing a predator is more likely to lead a species to extinction than introducing one, the classic case being the removal of the mountain lion from the Kaibab National Park in the US. The kaibab deer then had a population explosion followed by a dramatic collapse. Before the cat was introduced into Australia there had already been several major changes in the predator–prey relations, especially the introduction of the dingo and the disappearance of the thylacine in mainland Australia, and one other major predator, the Aborigine, was disempowered at about the same time that the feral cats achieved their near-continental distribution, so one might see the cat at least in part as filling a newly vacant or under-tenanted niche.

What seems more likely than that cats have either been major agents of marsupial mayhem or that they have not been at all significant is that cats have been a serious threat to some species in some places. They are certainly a major hazard in attempting to re-colonise parts of the Peron Peninsula with small marsupials, but Tim would concede this, although not, it seems, Dr Walmsley's comparable efforts. The rangers I knew in the Snowy River National Park were convinced that cats were a real threat to the survival of the lyre-bird in that area, once apparently fairly common. Nevertheless, they survive in quasi-suburban Sherbrooke Forest, so even with birds there is contrary evidence. Where we live in Perth (one of Australia's gigantic urban feedlots, as Flannery calls them) there has been a spectacular revival, to my delight, of several ground-feeding bird species, especially the willie-wagtail and the mudlark. Their local disappearance was caused by inappropriate pesticide use, and their recolonisation has not at all been impeded by the moggies. This, of course, like so much of the evidence, is anecdotal, but at least from someone who is neither a cat-lover nor a cat-hater.

Pyrophobia

Flannery comes close to endorsing a beautiful lie himself, although it is a corrective exaggeration rather than a lie, and he illustrated this in *The Future Eaters*. Some early colonists and explorers in south-eastern Australia remarked on the skill with which the Aborigines used fire as a maintenance tool. Sylvia Hallam showed, largely through linguistic analysis, that the Nyoongah had a sophisticated understanding of fire-management in south-western Australia. Rhys Jones, with the all the flair of a top advertising executive, popularised the concept with the phrase "fire-stick farming", and this became an invaluable counter to the common view at the time that the Aborigines were primitive savages. So far so good, but as Flannery has remarked elsewhere, in such a highly politicised arena the moderate view loses out. Without in the least discrediting Aboriginal knowledge of fire-management, there is reason to doubt its universal application; indeed, it strains credulity to think of a population about the size of Perth applying fire-hazard reduction (control) burning over a continent. They would have had time for nothing else, and as in all communities there would have been a few irresponsibles whose fire escaped, other mishaps from sudden changes in wind direction, lightning strike and all those troubles that our own society struggles to cope with, often unsuccessfully, even with high-technology resources like the capacity for water bombing.

In any case, many areas of dense forest appear to have been virtually uninhabited. A.W. Howitt recorded some, like the gorge of the Mitchell, which was off-limits, and parts of East Gippsland. The Krautungalung of the lower Snowy area were not true nomads: they practised transhumance, moving in a defined territory from the coast, up river and back again in a repeated seasonal pattern. According to Howitt, they called the people of the sparsely inhabited dense forest to the east, "the Wild Men" (Brajerak). The Nyoongah of south-western Western Australia had a distribution pattern not unlike that of today: coastal, estuarine, along the rivers and in the light woodlands of what is today the wheatbelt, the terrain in which their management techniques were likely to be most effective. The heavy jarrah and karri forests of the Darling Plateau were sparsely inhabited, although Hallam does produce good evidence that they (or parts of them) were more open than they are today. Many other areas, in south-eastern Australia, of what is now fairly dense forest seem once to have been "open and park-like".

In central Australia, the anthropologist Tindale described the Aborigines, whose culture he admired, as "peripatetic pyromaniacs" capable of setting fire to thousands of square kilometres of *Triodia* to catch a few lizards – but they were true nomads, living with a different ecology. Flannery calls the colonists "pyro-phobic". People with phobias all sound a bit neurotic, but all settled societies are pyrophobic, as most Aboriginal societies seem to have been. That is why they managed fire to try to reduce its potentially destructive powers – just as French foresters, for example, have been doing in southern France for many years. None of the above is to challenge Flannery's central thesis, that large parts of Australia are more flammable now than they were two hundred years ago.

Immigration and cultural diversity

Flannery gives a rich account of the cultural diversity of the founding decades, which includes the Eora, but he then shows how the culture became progres-sively more introverted, persisting until the 1 9 5 0s. I have no disagreement with the broad-brush thesis, only a few more marginal notes. I am older than Tim, born in 1 9 2 7 and so with a different experience. My father was a country bank manager, and much of my youth was spent in Mildura. We lived above and behind the bank in one of the two main streets, Langtree Avenue, and I have no memory of xenophobia. A group of Chinese lived next door; they ran a laundry. We neither liked nor disliked them. They were different from us, but they were there, full stop. Mildura was the dream of two Americans, the Chaffey brothers. Ernestine Hill wrote a book about them and called it *Water into Gold*. I wrote a book with a chapter heading "Gold into Water", since the irrigation water for the whole irrigation area was described as "free", which meant that the huge infra-structure costs were not paid for by the consumer. Flannery gives the Chaffey brothers stick, and rightly so on environmental grounds. Oddly enough, howev-er, Mildura was a social success. Almost half my father's customers were Italians or others of Mediterranean origin, and this before World War II. There was no question of "acceptance": they were there (and they brought us great fruit and vegetables). It was the war that broke the social harmony. From Mildura we moved to Horsham, where many of (the best) farmers were German, come east from South Australia. Tim concedes that successive waves were absorbed, and this really strengthens his point rather than the reverse. There were, however, deep cul-tural divisions within those societies, between the Protestants (us) and the Irish Catholics, who were plotting to take over the place. Venom was also directed at the Jews, who were planning to do the same thing. There were cultural neuroses enough, but they may have varied from place to place. I doubt that Australia has ever been quite so homogeneous as superficial appearances suggest.

Food

I have some reservations about the globalisation of food, having spent a lot of time in Italy, where Italian cuisine is still resolutely Italian, with minor exceptions like pizza, essentially an American re-import in its present form, although there was an earlier Italian source. The main customers for it are tourists anyway, mostly American. I love Italian cooking, but there is nothing like the variety we enjoy here in Australia. Outside Paris, French food is still mostly French; outside south-east England, English food, alas, is still mostly English (and that includes the "Chinese" food). We have every right to be proud of the quality and diversity of our cuisine, as does New Zealand, and yes, it owes much to migration, as well as to the Australasian taste for travel.

Moo-cow Mitchell

It seems a pity to interrupt the grand sweep of the Flannery narrative with nit-picking, but quibbles do suggest themselves with such a thought-provoking essay. "Moo-cow" Mitchell's vision of settling 7 5,0 0 0 British migrants in the south-west of Western Australia did not fail because of "the truculent soils and the sheer weight of the forest to be disposed of". The latter was back-breaking, but the enterprise failed because the blocks were too small for subsistence farming, and much more important, because the only cash crop, milk and butter, had no real market. Transport was poor, refrigeration prohibitively expensive, and the domestic market minute. The "landscape of bucolic bliss" is there now, however, and it does combine a distinctively Australian quality with a kind of European civility – but the crop is not grass but wine-grapes, perhaps the most economically successful and sustainable agricultural enterprise in Western Australia. Get the crop and the market right! The remaining dairy farms make gourmet cheeses, which give a higher return and are easier to transport than bulk milk or butter.

The wine industry around Margaret River has been self-funded, much of it from the ample resources of the medical profession, and it is further supported by and supports the tourist industry. Mitchell's dairy farms were a state enterprise, and although the funding was meagre and the implementation largely failed, its failure actually paved the way for the vines, and Mitchell's principle should not be dismissed.

Grapevines win over grass on another count: they are deep-rooted, while grass and cereal crops are not. The future lies with the deep-rooted: salt-bush, tagasaste (very successful on the light lands around Jurien Bay), agro-forestry, reversion to natural scrub. *Acacia cyanopylla* has been planted in trials near Esperance. Sheep are naturally browsing rather than grazing animals, and the acacia is highly nutritious and nitrogenising to boot, but it demands more fencing and more management than current practice.

Much of the southern half of agricultural Australia is ill-suited to its current use, primarily large-scale cropping for cereal, mostly wheat. Productivity is very low by both European and North American standards when productivity is measured by yield per hectare. Italy has a total cereal production that is close to that of Australia and quite often exceeds it, from much less land. Twice in the last decade the United Kingdom (which effectively is East Anglia, the only part of the UK with a climate dry enough to ripen wheat) produced more wheat than Australia (admittedly two good years there and two bad years here). To put a few figures on it, in 1998/9, Australia had a wheat yield of 22.1 million tonnes (Mt) with a (comparatively meagre) yield of 1.91 t/ha. World production was 588 Mt, to which we contributed about one-thirtieth — although we exported nearly four-fifths of our production. That, however, was a very good year, the second best in the decade. Back in 1991/92 we produced 10.6 Mt against 90.6 for the EU: Germany and the UK produced considerably more, France more than three times as much, and even Italy almost as much, at 9.4 Mt (and for Italy, for all intents and purposes you can read Sicily). The story was similar, even worse, in 1994/5, when we were down to 8.9 Mt. It is also worth emphasising that although our figures vary substantially from year to year, from a low of 8.9 to a high of 23.7 Mt (in 1996/97), the European figures are relatively constant: France always produces around 30 Mt. Figures for the other cereals tell a similar story but on a much smaller scale on our part. We produced 1.39 Mt of rice, about one-four-hundredth of world production, and exported about half. We also exported about half of our coarse grains production (primarily oats, barley, sorghum and maize), which represents about one-ninetieth of world production. The bottom line, which comes as a surprise to many, is that we are not a significant cereal producer on the global scale[1]. Our National Anthem is another beautiful lie: I have proposed an alternative.

Mining

Every now and then Australia or parts of it win the lottery. How the prize-money has been and is spent may be worth more attention than it has received. The prize has come from mineral discovery, and although Blainey's title *The Rush That Never Ended* (great book) has been true in the broad sense, it has not been continuous, but more like herpes, breaking out in different ways in different places. How have we spent the lottery wins? Victoria built some fine provincial cities, notably Ballarat, Bendigo and Castlemaine, and it recklessly overbuilt its mega-feedlot, marvellous Melbourne, which then crashed. It began Melbourne's primacy as an industrial and financial centre; the industry worked while we had tariff protection and the financial control until Sydney caught the new waves of information technology and left Melbourne to its conservative ways.

Western Australia won a later lottery in the last decade of the nineteenth century and spent heavily on infrastructure: Fremantle Port, railways, and a reticulated water system to the south-west and a pipeline to Kalgoorlie. This is over-simplified, but there is a point: the intention was to invest in the state's future, translated as its agricultural productivity. Salinity has seen to it that this hasn't worked much better than the moo-cows, but it was a good try.

Today we have won the lottery again, repeatedly, in the Pilbara, where the magnificent infrastructure has been built by the mining companies themselves. It will not outlast them, however, because without mining it will have limited alternative functions. Most of the money that has poured into state coffers has gone into general revenue and has been spent on doubling the size of Western Australia's principal feedlot, Perth.

Mining creates skills as well as wealth. It needs emphasising that it generates and supports much of the "knowledge industry" in Australia, through the technological sophistication of the offshore oil rigs, the plant at the Burrup Peninsula and the facilities at Port Hedland, where the mainframe computer is more powerful than the space control centre at Cape Canaveral. All of the above are not only leading-edge technology by world standards. They also require constant input from highly skilled personnel, as does marketing and management of such global enterprises. Much of the employment is in Perth and the other state capitals. If we are to have a "knowledge nation", this is the most likely driver.

Mining is not discussed by Flannery, and is anathema to many "conservationists", for two or three reasons. One is a fear of all multinationals, irrespective of their individual character. There is hostility based on the appalling environmental degradation of early mining in Australia, which continued well into the last century. There are still rogues, but the main players are now, for the most part, exemplary. There is minimal land disruption compared to agriculture and grazing, and they are among the major employers of anthropologists, biologists and re-vegetation experts. The other fear is that they deal in an exhaustible resource and their activities are unsustainable. This is both true and misleading. The known reserves of all our major mineral resources are greater now than they were thirty years ago; in a sense new technologies "create" resources. New techniques of exploration will, without doubt, locate major ore bodies that now lie beneath the thick regolith of weathering products (including a thick sand blanket) that covers so much of central Australia, thus concealing surface indicators of mineralisation. This has hitherto not been penetrable by conventional methods of exploration, but CSIRO has been working on new techniques with great possibilities. One is the Glass Earth Project, which will allow us to "see" below the top kilometre of the earth's surface by using magnetic fields, gravity, infra-red surface observations and computer modelling. Concealed ore deposits, like the bedrock sequences in which they lie, are highly weathered in much of Australia, and their appearance, mineralogy and chemistry are radically altered to the point that neither surface observation nor remote sensing can detect them.

These techniques are now being used in terrain "previously opaque to exploration". There is good reason to believe that vastly more mineral deposits await discovery than relatively crude exploration technology has discovered to date. This is good news in that mining is one of the relatively few things other than cricket and tennis that we do well by global standards, and we need the money. How we spend it becomes the important question.

The Dead Hand

Flannery exposes some of the limitations of the "environmental" movement, and his essay is a telling critique of Amanda Lohrey's preceding essay on the Greens. Campaigns to "save" gems of the environment have been useful and at times successful, to our benefit, but they do not adequately address the fundamental issues of land use and land management, or in Flannery's words, "land, soil and biodiversity conservation".

Flannery cites Jock Marshall's *The Great Extermination: A Guide to Australian Cupidity, Wickedness and Waste*. It was an important book, and it should be in the library of every secondary school in the country. But Marshall was the original shock-jock. I would put beside it, along with Watkin Tench, *The Future Eaters* and a few other key texts, Bruce Davidson's book *Australia: Wet or Dry*, which should be reprinted.

Flannery is a mammalian biologist by trade, and from Monash, hence his affinity for Marshall. For mammalian biologists, "biodiversity" has become a mantra. It matters immensely, and I can share his grief at the loss of the white-footed rabbit-rat or Gnar-ruck, just as I share that of the Greens over the loss of Lake Pedder (in the latter case, from direct experience). We are the poorer for both, but neither loss keeps me awake at night, whereas the increasing salination of our soils is the stuff of nightmare. There is something to be said for Phillip Baxter's image of life-boat Australia after all, not so much in fending off the hands of those struggling to climb on board (although that too, alas) but primarily in deciding what to jettison from the sinking ship. "Triage" is a useful concept because it focuses the mind on the essential or key issue, which in our case is the land. This is the danger of all the "save" campaigns. Worthy in themselves, they divert attention from the core problems. What I want us to save is the viability of Australia.

An attack on salinity will also be our best approach to conserving biodiversity, both animal and vegetable, by preserving or maintaining habitat, rather than by campaigning to "save" this or that species. The latest report from the National Land and Water Resources Audit predicts that salinity will impinge not only on our agricultural land. Some two million hectares of native vegetation are at risk, as are many wetlands. To reverse or halt this process, to restore at least one-third of our agricultural land to shrub and woodland and to dramatically reduce stocking rates on pastoral rangelands will be necessary to maintain some food production, but it will achieve the re-creation of animal habitat as a by-product. National parks won't do it: one of the most telling of Flannery's telling phrases is that they have become "marsupial ghost towns".

Population, immigration, decency

The last section deals with population policies, for which "stocking rates" is a useful phrase to link environmental and social concerns. I need no convincing that we need to reduce immigration rates very substantially, nor that we must somehow reconcile this with our humanitarian responsibilities. Phrases like "creating the greatest good for the greatest number" will not help in achieving this. If you have one hundred dollars and one hundred people, you can give them all one dollar, thus helping the greatest number, or you can give the hundred dollars to one person, who gets the greatest good, or you can give fifty people two dollars or whatever ratio takes your fancy. Academic niggling aside, however, I am very much with Flannery about population growth, the need for a more humane society, and a better expression of this through foreign policy. Vietnam was a sorry mistake. Iraq was not our war. Most of our aid goes to Papua New Guinea, but we have had great difficulty in ensuring that it is effectively used (having assisted in a couple of ADAB surveys of our foreign aid programs, I know how hard it is to get good results, with all the dedication and goodwill in the world). Our intervention in Timor seems to have been our success story so far, but it will be a continuing responsibility, and I would like to see a fair proportion of our limited resources directed there.

This is contemporary politics. The main force of this powerful essay is to detail the extent of the environmental crisis, and in this it is exemplary. If at times the Flannery rhetoric has overtones that suggest the Pontifex Maximus and a new Messiah, so be it. We need ritual cleansing (of woolly thinking) and we need saving – which leads me to a last despairing question. Is anyone listening?

George Seddon

1. Data from 1999 *Australian Commodity Statistics*, Australian Bureau of Agricultural and Resource Economics, Canberra

Barney Foran

It is easy to be romanced by Tim Flannery's engaging polemic, the turn of phrase, the millennium captured in a single phrase and the catholicity of his tastes in history, peoples, politics and science. It is the sort of essay that people read to each other savouring a word sequence, delighting in a well-thrust dagger and captured by a range of ecological insights that only a well-trod traveller in time can bring. A scientist examining Flannery's huge canvas could easily become pedantic and lose the broad thrust and forget Flannery's role as a provocateur. Instead I'll adopt a role similar to Flannery's, put the data to one side and present my own polemic where he left off.

Australia does not have a water problem, a biodiversity problem and a population problem as Tim Flannery suggests. In reality our environmental problems are driven by a protracted trade problem and an affluence problem. Most national policy churn and environmental hand-wringing is aimed at ameliorating the knock-on effects of these primary drivers rather than attacking the causes directly.

First to trade! Because of history, location and preference we have locked ourselves into paying for imports by trading in food, fibre, minerals and some manufactured products. True, we are increasing our trading acumen with wine to Europe, cars to Saudi Arabia and farmed tuna to Japan, giving great copy for ministers of both persuasions telling us how bright we've become since the Hawke and Keating era modernised our economy. But beautiful lies abound. For every one billion dollars in hard-won car exports we still import three billion dollars worth of flash transport from Japan and Germany, so preserving a three-to-one imports-to-exports ratio that has been with us for some time. Generally, we have locked ourselves into high energy and water transaction costs for every hard-won export dollar. We wonder, myopically, why our inland rivers are becoming saline drains and why we are derided by most countries for our greenhouse emission profligacy and our Kyoto non-compliance.

Perhaps one solution lies in finding alternative methods of trade exchange such as bartering, rather than writing our trade contracts in dollars, yen or euros that in the end discount the value of an Australian dollar. Australia exports more water in net terms (embodied in traded goods) than we supply to our cities and towns. Prices are set in world terms, economists talk about comparative and competitive advantage, and every Christmas time our national dailies promote the "water crisis" while ministers meet and Wentworth Groups advise. Trade goes almost unmentioned, although local papers take twice-yearly swipes at rice and cotton growers as though they were the cause, rather than the symptom, of the problem. The import bill may have to adjust radically because the environmental account is, seemingly, always in the red.

Water-poor countries abound, some with items that we require and pay lots for. Saudi Arabia (oil), Korea (manufactures) and Singapore (computers and musical instruments) are all surprisingly water-poor on a per capita basis. In twenty years' time we may exchange goods on the basis of the environmental services embodied in them rather than using a financial rate of exchange. Barter could be catching.

Alternatively, if world trade attributed environmental negatives to the country of consumption rather than the country of production, then the parlous state of local environmental accounts could be sheeted home to the consciences of consumers in downtown Singapore, Los Angeles and Tokyo. However, our greenhouse account still stays in the red, since what we lose in exporting the emissions with the aluminium will return in spades, embodied in consumer electronics and fancy cars.

Then on to personal affluence, the central driver of Australia's trade problem. Flannery is correct when he says that the more people, the more problems, because technology cannot deliver a big enough finger to stop the flood from the dyke. It does not matter whether the consumer is black, white or brindle, a consumer is still a consumer. Technology tends to produce as many environmental problems as it solves. As a race, humankind delights in newness and difference. When there are no paddocks to plough, no forests to fell and no web pages to design, we salve our beleaguered spirits with a trip to the shopping mall or the e-commerce portal. Consumption and affluence makes us feel good, it makes jobs and it makes the economy grow. It is a brave commentator who would question this way of living.

Beautiful lies abound in terms like "sustainable consumption". We are kept busy sorting our rubbish for the recycling bin without really knowing whether the wheelie bin culture provides any net benefit in energy and material terms.

We could find out, if we wanted. We could design society as a new-age chemical plant where every output is an input to another cycle, another product or another service. But urban Australia is a rather anarchical beast and perhaps we'd lose the magic of the pizza shop and the eternal car yard if we attempted to implement some grand design. The thought that we might consider some top-down overall design which intersected with some bottom-up consumer action is a rather heavy concept that smacks of a centrally planned economy. Let the market fix itself!

But could we ever change and would we want to? I remember a discussion at a conference about Sustainable Seattle. It started with an urban stormwater problem caused by intense thunder-pumps and too many hard surfaces. The Seattle engineers found that tree-scapes (slowing down the water) were more effective than concrete drains. When the streets were treed, the people came back, the neighbourhoods and their local shops emerged, people walked on the streets, the streets were safe and people had a life again apart from cable TV and the blank stare of the shopping mall. At a micro-scale this is happening in some suburban blocks in Australia. But it is local government stuff and seemingly what the people want. Unfortunately it's not the stuff of how you'd run a "real" country.

But somehow we have to substitute the rush and excitement of a real life for the rush brought on by buying and owning things. Flannery's picture of "mothers with grown-up families wanting to save whales and forests" is fascinating. But how do we turn ardent corporate managers into consumption misers who care more for clean air and clean water than a corporate spreadsheet and a profitable bottom line?

To supplement Flannery's eight coda items, here are six physical realities that are precursors to beating the beautiful lies at their own game.

Reality one is that the composition of Australia's international trade is what drives environmental decline. We need to foment a revolution in what we grow and, most importantly, in what goods we are prepared to trade.

Reality two is that shortening the production chain and bringing the producers and consumers into physical proximity could bring many social and environmental issues into confluence. This does not mean building jumbo jets and advanced computers in the local community hall. But it may mean vegetables and fruit becoming seasonal again, so that I won't be able to buy Californian grapefruit in Esperance in the middle of an Australian summer.

Reality three is that the prices we pay for many sorts of food in Australia may have to change appreciably because of the water, land and energy impost of the current production systems. Current ideology sees that this price increase should be levied at the production base or at the farm gate. Other ideologies see that the polluter-pays principle can equally be applied to the consumer in the grand sweep of things where the individual consumer is both the driver of the economy as well as ultimate recipient of all the goods and services that it produces. What about a cappuccino tax to pay for the water and greenhouse cost of the milk production chain?

Reality four is that urban Australia is directly responsible for the parlous state of Australia's environmental quality. Urban demand for cheap services and products from Australian landscapes is a primary driver. Of equal importance is urban imports which in turn put more pressure on the farm and the mine to balance our external trading account under the current structure and functioning of the Australian economy.

Reality five is that corporate and government managers are running a marathon with blindfolds when it comes to key infrastructure and machine stocks that determine how Australia works physically. These stocks determine our long-term future, they are slow moving and turn over every fifty years or so. Yet we implement first-home-owner schemes without any cross-compliance requirements for greenhouse emissions. We sink billions of dollars of industry assistance into the Australian car industry without the requirement that they produce hybrid-engined cars that all government fleets are required to purchase.

Reality six is that urban Australia, home to three-quarters of our citizens, is becoming critically energy-dependent and lacks the robustness and resilience to deal with energy shocks that will be with us from 2020 onwards unless we start a revolutionary response tomorrow. Each year the fossil fuel industries in Australia receive six billion dollars of subsidy and we still buy the story that in general renewable energy is not price-competitive and that the propellers of wind-power generators kill endangered bird species.

Perhaps the biggest lie of all, foisted on us by the national spin doctors, is that economic growth forever, at a rate of 3−4% per annum, could ever be compatible with the concept of environmental sustainability. For every consumption dollar that I spend in today's Australian economy, I cause the use of thirty-seven litres of water, I use the energy equivalent of one quarter of a litre of petrol and I stimulate three square metres of land disturbance.

If Australians are to "rescue the future" and refute most of the beautiful lies, urgent and direct action is required on three fronts.

The first is to acknowledge that every consumption dollar has an impact. Much is heard of the many benefits that flow from each additional dollar, but somehow the negatives are always someone else's problem. Tim Flannery gets the lie just right when he describes the "sheep-carrying-capacity story" that was ascribed to Minister Ruddock by the *Australian's* Paul Kelly. So consumption dollars are great and we all love them. However, we'd better start labelling each of them so that we can judge for ourselves whether the downstream effects of a hundred-kilometre car journey, a kilogram of beef and a litre of wine are just the gift we had in mind for our children's children.

The second is to change the footing of the Australian economy from promoting personal consumption to encouraging investment into brainpower, robust communities, urban infrastructure and repairing the farm and the river. National income must be derived from investments into fine design and great ideas rather than bulk consumption. Currently $600 billion in superannuation funds is slopping around the system looking for a place to work. The investment community tell me that good projects are few, apart from a few one-offs such as buying Sydney Airport and building yet another connector ring road to join one node of congestion to another.

The third is to start valuing people as solutions rather than relying on technological wizardry. Technology can certainly help us stall many of the effects promoted by the beautiful lies. But for many environmental challenges, technological solutions are like bandaids and aspirins for a broken leg. We need to get past the symptoms and attack the real cause of the pain.

Rescuing the future from the current trajectory we appear to be on is the most urgent task facing Australia. Flannery despairs that we have frittered away the opportunities that Federation brought us a hundred years ago. Long-term population modelling[1] tells us that we have a twenty-year window of unparalleled good fortune before past indecision will catch up with us. While in 2020 Australia will not turn into a pumpkin, it is then that we will start our slide into ageing, arable land loss, oil depletion and river salinity. We can avoid the worst effects of these, but do we have the courage?

Now is the time to create an era that we could be proud of, when we fixed up the place. The next ten years will tell.

Barney Foran

1. See Barney Foran and Franzi Poldy, *Future Dilemmas: Options to 2050 for Australia's Population, Technology, Resources and Environment*, November 2002,
   http://www.cse.csiro.au/research/program5/futuredilemmas

A. Duncan Brown

There is little with which to disagree in the main thrust of Tim Flannery's *Quarterly Essay*, *Beautiful Lies*, but a number of specific points do need some qualification, usually because they over-simplify very complex situations or processes.

The Aboriginal practice of burning scrub or forest is frequently cited by Flannery as a justification for the current policy of "hazard reduction" burning. A problem with this argument is that no one knows how frequently any particular area of land was burnt by the Aborigines, at least in eastern Australia. There is some continuation of the practice in parts of the Northern Territory and of Western Australia where, of course, environmental conditions are very different from those in the east. The statistics for the effectiveness of hazard reduction burning are fuzzy – needless to say. What they suggest is that the practice increases the frequency of low-intensity fires (because it causes them), decreases the frequency of fires of medium intensity, but has no effect on the frequency or severity of high-intensity ("blow up") fires. In the light of that, and taking into account the extent of European impact on the Snowy Mountains and, of course, the appalling weather conditions during the January 2003 fires, to imply that the possible extinction of the pygmy possum and the corroboree frog can be attributed to lack of hazard reduction burning is to draw a very long bow indeed. Similarly, I have serious reservations about his suggestion that the cessation of burning by Aborigines "is the major cause of mammal extinction in central Australia" – not least because of the complexity of any ecosystem and the length of time involved.

Flannery notes that over the past few decades the Royal National Park in NSW has "lost its kangaroos, its koalas, its platypus and greater gliders" and uses this as evidence against "proclaiming more such reserves". The arguments for and against nature reserves are not nearly as simple as that statement suggests. It is now generally acknowledged that if a reserve is to sustain its biodiversity, it must have an area greater than a certain minimum, a minimum that obviously will vary with the type of environment in which the reserve is located. In addition, wherever possible, there should be "corridors" connecting neighbouring reserves and allowing movement of animals between them. Not only is Sydney's Royal National Park Australia's oldest national park, it is one of the smallest in the country. It adjoins a city. Its borders, being the sea, Port Hacking and a major highway, are essentially impassable to the relevant animals. Internally, it is bisected by a major road and further fragmented by smaller ones. It is an obvious example of inadequacy and cannot be used as a valid argument against the principle of national parks.

Flannery argues in support of the "kangaroo industry". Part of his argument is that it is less cruel to shoot a kangaroo through the head than to put cattle through the ordeals to which they are exposed on farms and their subsequent slaughter in an abattoir. I would add that the comparison is even more stark if the cattle have been raised in a feedlot. But there are some qualifications at this level. One is that the marksmen are as good as this comparison implies and do not leave wounded kangaroos to die slowly. Another is that the kangaroos that are shot are not mothers with dependent joeys.

There is another less emotional dimension to the comparison which Flannery does not address. Kangaroos grow faster and reach maturity sooner than cattle – slightly over two years for kangaroos compared with about four years (including gestation period) for cattle. This implies that kangaroos will withdraw nutrients from their ecosystem – and hence from their soil – faster than the same mass of cattle. Under most conditions in a natural ecosystem this would not matter because the elements are recycled within the system. In commercial agriculture, however, the produce is consumed elsewhere. In other words, weight for weight, and depending on the age at which the cattle are slaughtered, harvesting kangaroos will normally impoverish soil faster than harvesting cattle from the same environment. Because of many variables, and the qualifications that would follow, I am reluctant to quantify this statement in a short letter such as this.

Commercial agriculture is possible only through the application of fertiliser – but that is not "sustainable" because some nutrient elements are used in a manner that is essentially irreversible. The element most obviously vulnerable to exhaustion is phosphorus. I should emphasise here that, while this has particularly serious implications for Australia, it is a global problem. Calculating the "life expectancy" of natural resources has many uncertainties, of course. My own estimates indicate that, if present trends continue, known global phosphorus resources will be exhausted within 8 5 to 1 9 0 years.[1] A long time in the perspective of politicians and captains of industry, but a very short time indeed on evolutionary, or even historical, time scales.

I find Flannery's arguments in support of whaling somewhat short of convincing. Having argued previously for a kangaroo industry partly on the basis of the cruelty of slaughtering cattle, he makes no mention of the inherent cruelty of harpooning. From my perspective, this is even more difficult to justify when the result of that form of slaughter is used, at least in Japan, not to help sustain a population but rather to titillate the rich.

In the context of whaling, Flannery acknowledges the complexity of natural systems. In the paragraphs that follow, however, he proceeds to comment on old-growth forests on the one hand and biodiversity, soil degradation and water conservation on the other as if the two areas are unrelated. Most of Australia's soil degradation and problems with water, to say nothing of loss of biodiversity, are largely a consequence of deforestation.

A. Duncan Brown

1. See A. Duncan Brown, *Feed or Feedback: Agriculture, Population Dynamics and the State of the Planet*, Utrecht, International Books, in press.

Peter Christoff

Tim Flannery's ecological humanism is fundamental to this essay and to the ways in which it challenges "the lies we tell about land and people". Flannery rightly highlights the persistence in practice of the founding myth of *terra nullius* and the potentially "fatal mismatch" between the "colonial insert" of European attitudes and practices and the ecological and cultural realities of this country and its original inhabitants. Echoing Bill Clinton's comment while visiting Australia during the *Tampa* crisis – that he couldn't understand the fuss over 4 0 0 refugees when climate change could deliver another 4 0 0 , 0 0 0 if we didn't change our patterns of consumption – Flannery is right to argue that, "If things do not change, it will become more and more difficult to sustain even the number of people we now have, let alone take the vast number of refugees our foreign policy threatens to create in the days ahead". "The old nexus between unsustainable dreams, environmental damage and population growth" must be broken, he writes.

His eco-humanism infuses his position on population and the environment at the essay's end. "Australia, as we have seen, is labouring under the burden of a profound environmental crisis for which there is no solution in sight … at current levels of consumerism and technological capacity, the continent has too many people". Nevertheless, he argues passionately, and rightly, that we cannot adopt a "lifeboat Australia" policy. We must continue to take refugees – for which our foreign policy has made us morally responsible – but do so in the context of a sustainable population policy that will regulate future immigration.

Yet Flannery's version of eco-humanism is also problematic. It leads him to advocate a narrowly anthropocentric view of how nature should be made to work for humans. It misdirects his criticisms of Australian environmentalism. Ultimately, it undermines his opposition to "the old nexus".

Flannery is a practised and practising controversialist. Too often, for the sake of stirring hyperbole and in the absence of basic research that might tame a good iconoclastic assertion, he tosses out the bilby with the bathwater. As a result, his essay is often frustrating and infuriating. Frustrating because it offers only a cursory and fragmentary view of Australia's critical environmental problems: Flannery devotes nine pages in total to water use, salinity and climate change, yet gives five pages to the problem of the feral cat. And infuriating because of its glib misrepresentation of the Australian environment movement.

His discussion of the feral cat reveals problems that plague the work as a whole: it is too often poorly researched, its argument is too often based on simplification and inference from a single but inappropriate example, and too often it is hard to draw meaningful conclusions from that argument.

Just consider this brief quote concerning feral felines: "One museum curator has reported, in condemning the cat as a major menace, that felines kill billions of native animals each year. It's a frightening figure that has led many to see cats as major contributors to Australia's biodiversity crisis. Yet is the moggy really responsible for the extinction of Australian natives? Clearly cats are efficient predators ... Yet beyond their hunting finesse, there is little evidence that cats have exterminated any species in the Australian environment." For added emphasis, Flannery asserts that only one native species, the white-footed rabbit-rat, is likely to have been exterminated by cats.

Here we slide from an accurate description of predator impact to the unsupported suggestion that many (but who?) believe the moggy is not only a contributor to but *responsible for* multiple extinctions ... which Flannery denies. He goes on to ask, "How to reconcile this information with the dogmatic belief of some environmentalists that cats are a major – if not *the* major – threat to Australian wildlife?"

Well, nothing he has said shows this belief to be wrong. The commonly available and authoritative review of relevant scientific literature, Dickman's *Overview of the Impacts of Feral Cats on Australian Native Fauna*, published in 1 9 9 6, also attributes the extinction of four other species – Gould's mouse, the Alice Springs mouse, the Darling Downs hopping-mouse and the big-eared hopping mouse – directly to feral cats, which in addition have contributed substantially to the decline of seventeen other native mammal, seven bird and three reptile species. Flannery too, a few pages later, confirms the widely held view that cats, alongside a multitude of other factors, *contribute to* impacts on vulnerable populations of native mammals.

In all, he first attributes simplistic views to others and then "retrieves" the situation by offering blatantly obvious "complexity". Ultimately there is nothing exceptionable here. The "argument" is merely the yowl of a straw cat.

Indeed, what conclusion are we to draw? Should we do nothing about feral cats, cane toads, rabbits or foxes, which *alone* may not have caused the extinction of many native species but collectively are major contributors? Are we to believe that more than a few environmentalists are always wrong about the environment, as he seems to suggest? Flannery's point – whatever it may be – remains furtive and lost in the undergrowth.

By far the most problematic part of the essay, for me, is the section called "The Dead Hand". Anyone familiar with Australian environmentalists and environmental campaigns would struggle to recognise them in Flannery's reductive caricature of the movement as a bunch of tree-huggers, animal liberationists and naive, narrow-minded preservationists. I will deal first with what is offered in the essay and then add what is missing from this account.

Flannery indicates that he is writing about the goals of the "early conservation movement" (a movement that for him begins in the late 1 9 6 0s and early 1 9 7 0s, although many others, such as Hutton and Connor in their *History of the Australian Environment Movement*, rightly locate the first wave of conservationism in the nineteenth century). But he then proceeds ahistorically: early movement understandings and aims are confusingly attributed to a very different movement existing three or more decades later.

For example, he suggests the early movement's desire to "save" nature in national parks or reserves was central to a strategy to conserve biodiversity. The Australian national parks movement, which dates from the 1 9 3 0s and was first championed by the likes of Miles Dunphy, initially sought to establish national parks for aesthetic and recreational reasons. It wasn't until the 1 9 8 0s and 1 9 9 0s that its organisational advocates transformed their aims, and parks and reserves came to be seen as a vital aspect – but never the sole focus – of a strategic approach to the conservation of native species (biodiversity).

Nevertheless, Flannery castigates the movement's push for nature reserves, arguing that, "If we look around our national parks today, what we see in the great majority of cases are marsupial ghost-towns, which preserve only a tiny fraction of the fauna that was there in abundance two centuries ago" and citing the Royal National Park south of Sydney as a classic example. Really? Like many early reserves, the relatively small Royal National Park – our oldest park, established in 1 8 7 9 – was never "designed" as a biodiversity reserve but created for recreation, "for the use of the public forever". Does Flannery's argument apply equally to Kakadu, the Daintree or the Mallee? No environmentalist would argue that even a complete suite of national parks, one representing a proportion of each major ecosystem, would be *sufficient* to the task of biodiversity preservation.

And what alternative is Flannery offering? No more parks? Would mining, logging or clearing these areas or subjecting them to other versions of "multiple use" be a better proposition?

The argument about whether or not nature reserves are the answer to the problem of biodiversity protection is rightly extended into a broader discussion of whether the Australian environment, sculpted by 6 0 , 0 0 0 years of indigenous hunting and fire-use, can indeed be preserved by being "locked up": "To think that we can walk away from managing the new environment that this history has created is a form of madness." Here again Flannery seems to suggest – inaccurately – that most environmentalists support a policy of absolute neglect, that little active management of national parks occurs (this will be a surprise to the various state environment departments, no doubt), and that all greenies are basically animal liberationists.

"It is in this context that we need to examine another focus of the Australian conservation movement – the preservation of native species," he writes. But what manner of preservation? Perhaps, just as "the black hunters culled the wildlife of Australia and preserved what was viable", we too should engage in culling and managing native species. The debate over culling has been a peripheral issue for much of the movement for the past forty years. Presently, environmentalists and green groups support a wide range of positions, from the wholesale pastoral use of kangaroos instead of cattle and sheep through to an absolute prohibition on the killing of native species. Nevertheless, most agree that preservation of native biodiversity requires very active management indeed – including management of feral plants and animals, use of fire, culling and co-ordinated activities on private and public land. Sadly, there is nothing in this essay that reflects on the complexity – or criticises the inadequacies of – current land management practices, biodiversity strategies and contemporary government or environment organisation policies and practices in relation to these matters.

It is when Flannery looks at whaling that the logic, the moral foundations and the underlying problem of his version of eco-humanism are most visible. "In order to maintain the blanket no-kill approach, the campaign to 'save the whales' has had to depart from *a strictly environmental logic*," he argues (emphasis added). "Because the whaling industry is so comparatively well managed, good environmental managers should be calling for the closure of a lot of other fisheries before they even begin to think about whales". Indeed, if whales "are closer in intelligence to the sheep than the dog, is it morally wrong to eat them if they can be harvested sustainably?"

How are we to understand all this? Flannery's discussion of whaling suggests that he rests comfortably among those who accept that anything and everything may be turned into a resource for human use, if only it can be done "sustainably". He even appears to support whaling while reflecting that we still don't know what has caused the recovery of a potential target species, the southern right whale. This argument places Flannery firmly among those boosters and developers who would claim sustainability and take the lot ... those whom he opposes elsewhere in the essay.

There is a chasm between the "old" resource conservationists (including Flannery) and the "new" environmentalists who argue that a vast range of other values must be recognised as valid reasons for preserving species and landscapes. Since the 1970s, the "new" environment movement has become the domain of many who are capable of discovering more in nature than a supermarket of resources. Whales are revered by some not because they may be an almost endless source of sheepish sea-steaks but because they are the planet's largest living creatures. Others are drawn to the awesome mystery of an animal that is truly global in its range. Whales are defended by still others because the whales' near-miss with extinction, their survival and slow recovery as a species, symbolise the hope that through public pressure other things too may be rescued from the brink – no point in fighting for the Tasmanian Tiger or Passenger Pigeon now. Similarly, forests may be one person's firewood but another's "green cathedral". Whales and forests have long been iconic rallying points for a broader cultural trend towards respecting and protecting nature, as well as part of the push to better understand and husband natural resources. That is why Greenpeace's symbolic as well as practical fight against whaling is part of its larger international campaign to stop the wanton plundering of global marine fisheries in toto. I suspect Flannery's narrow and instrumental view of what constitutes "good environmentalism" blinds him to these irreducible aspects of aesthetic and spiritual wonder, and also to their political consequences.

When one looks in detail at recent Australian environmental history, one sees just how diaphanously thin this essay really is. Perhaps it is Tim's narrow view of what is *strictly environmental* that encourages him to simplify the organisational and ideological complexity of much of an environment movement that has some 500,000 members and supporters, clustered in thousands of groups locally and nationally.

Perhaps too, as a result, the critical problems of defining what an environmentalist is and where the boundaries of the environment movement lie are avoided. The former environment minister Robert Hill once highlighted the definitional difficulties posed by the broad shift towards a "light green" culture in industry, civil society and government alike when he claimed that, "We are all greenies now." Certainly, the essay pays almost no attention to the institutionalisation of environmental concerns in government and industry action and is therefore silent on both the few strengths and the many weaknesses of such incorporation as it touches on critical issues like biodiversity preservation, climate change and land degradation.

Perhaps it is also why no mention is made of the Australian environment movement's extensive campaigning on and contributions to a range of not-so-flashy issues from the late 1980s onwards – the debates on economic restructuring and ecologically sustainable development, on the impacts of trade and farming on the environment, on industrial change and environmental modernisation in the manufacturing and transport sectors, on energy production and energy use, on urban planning, on waste production and disposal, on pollution and, most recently, on the over-use of water. Where in this essay is there discussion of the decade-long struggle over greenhouse and climate-change policy, or of the long history of the partnership between the Australian Conservation Foundation and the National Farmers' Federation that led firstly to the creation of the nationwide Landcare program with its over 3000 groups combating land degradation, including salinity, and then to Coastcare Australia? The strong support given by key national environmental organisations – the Australian Conservation Foundation, Friends of the Earth and the Wilderness Society in particular – to indigenous rights and Aboriginal co-management of national parks and other lands, including through revising the notion of wilderness to recognise indigenous ownership and prior and current use, also fails to get an airing.

Yet despite these minor omissions, Flannery answers his own question, "How are we to characterise the environment movement of the late twentieth century?" by saying that the movement has shifted "away from a focus on sustainability and towards subjectively emotional issues such as animal rights and tall trees… [campaigns which] with the best will in the world, actually run counter to good environmental management". Ultimately, I find it difficult not to read this essay as, in part, an uninformed attack on the environment movement.

Peter Christoff

[This letter was received too close to publication for Tim Flannery to respond.]

Tim Flannery

Beautiful lies continue to be unearthed, even in *Quarterly Essays*, so I am grateful to George Seddon, Barney Foran and A. Duncan Brown for taking the time to pen their thoughtful responses to my essay.

As always, George Seddon's words are beacons. There is much in his contribution that I wished I had written myself. His thoughts on Aboriginal fire-management are particularly valuable for setting out with clarity a general pattern that I have only otherwise glimpsed. This is that "firestick farming" was practised most assiduously on the more populated woodlands and plains. The tall timber country of the far south-east and south-west was, in contrast, lightly settled, where it was settled at all. Dense forests and their inhabitants were evidently regarded with ambivalence, and here fire frequency might have been dictated more by nature than man. And of course firestick farming was not a perfect system. But over **47,000** years, even lackadaisical application of the firestick can have a profound effect.

Seddon's first-hand recollection of the cultural milieu of rural Australia between the wars is invaluable. His sense of peaceful, albeit somewhat separate, co-existence of Chinese, English and others in places like Mildura begs explanation in light of earlier colonial experience. And of course he is correct that old-world obsessions with religion and British regional origins flourished in the new continent. Otherwise Ned Kelly would be a historical nobody.

Barney Foran takes the tack I had hoped for – both uncovering my own beautiful lies and building on my essay in important ways. His rigorous economic and environmental analysis, which suggests that Australia should not trade in low-value agricultural commodities, is indisputably correct. But how is such an eventuality to be arrived at? Likewise his view that life in the modern human feedlot is not all it could be has much to recommend it. But how, precisely, are we to escape this humdrum consumer existence? Here, surely, are key directions for future informed debate on Australian society.

A. Duncan Brown's contribution disappointed me somewhat in that he seems to misunderstand some of what I've written. His assertion that I am Tuckey-like in opposing the creation of more reserved land in Australia is plainly wrong. I would like to see more reserves, but it is of tremendous importance that we better manage the reserves we already have. Royal National Park's fate in losing native species may be an extreme one, but the entire reserve system is in diabolical trouble in this regard. A far more pro-active stance, including large-scale, systematic and well-researched reintroduction programs, is vital to maintaining small, isolated parks like Royal.

I find Duncan Brown's thoughts on soil impoverishment under kangaroo and cattle grazing curious. While kangaroos can be younger at harvest, they are also much smaller than cattle, and are of course harvested at varying ages. They also have a lower metabolic rate, making them more efficient at turning grass into meat. Though he posits an interesting thought, the argument is not sustained by rigorous analysis. His assertions on the humane aspects of whale harvesting are likewise limited: the "inherent cruelty of harpooning" versus shooting or throat-cutting is not evident to me. Surely all methods can lead either to slow and cruel, or swift and merciful deaths. We need more data here. His assertion that whale meat serves to "titillate the rich" of Japan rather than sustain a human population is baffling. If both are ecologically sustainable, is affluent titillation more base than bare subsistence? A moral and philosophical version of the Augean stables awaits the philosopher here.

Finally, I would like to comment on some comparisons that this essay has given birth to. I was somewhat dismayed by Christopher Pearson's ungenerous thought (voiced in the *Australian*) that perhaps I will be best remembered as Australia's own version of P. T. Barnum. I can only read this as an inference that he views my work as more show than substance. Such considered deafness to the arguments I have put has me empathising with Seddon's final question: "Is anybody listening?" But even George says I read like Pontifex Maximus, so perhaps the deliberately provocative style of QE9 has been misread by many as arrogance. Yet I hope that I have not shot so wide of the mark.

Tim Flannery

Peter Walsh

Amanda Lohrey's Groundswell: The Rise of the Greens makes two main points:
—The Greens are displacing the Democrats as the third party in Australian pol-
    itics as the Greens' policies are embraced by more and more electors; and
—Support for the major parties is steadily in decline.
Lohrey obviously welcomes that outcome and asserts it will improve public
policy and political morality. She is a "believer".
    I will examine her points in sequence.

The House of Representatives

In regard to the House of Representatives, figures scattered throughout the text
on the percentage of votes recorded by various parties are generally compatible
with the authoritative Parliamentary Library figures presented below in Table 1.

Table 1

Primary Vote – House of Representatives

Year	Labor	Lib./NP	Democrats	Greens	One Nation	Others
1983	49.48	43.61	5.03	N/A	N/A	1.16
1984	47.55	45.01	5.45	N/A	N/A	1.04
1987	45.83	46.07	6.03	N/A	N/A	1.66
1990	39.44	43.46	11.26	1.33	N/A	2.60
1993	44.92	44.27	3.75	1.85	N/A	3.11
1996	38.75	47.25	6.76	2.92	N/A	2.39
1998	40.10	39.51	5.13	2.62	8.43	1.91
2001	37.84	43.01	5.41	4.96	4.34	2.90

Source: Commonwealth of Australia Parliamentary Handbooks.

There is, however, one significant factual error, and also some contestable assumptions.

She states (correctly) that the major parties received 7 9.6 per cent of the primary vote in 1 9 8 8 and "approximately the same" in 2 0 0 1. In fact, the major party vote increased from 7 9.6 per cent to 8 0.8 5 per cent in 2 0 0 1. In this context an error of that size is important.

Secondly, there is the fact that One Nation came from nothing in 1 9 9 6 to be the biggest minor party (8.4 3 per cent) in 1 9 9 8, a year in which the Greens and Democrats vote went down. The minor party vote reached a record 1 6.1 8 per cent in 1 9 9 8. In 2 0 0 1, the One Nation vote fell by 4.0 9 per cent, the Democrats and Greens vote increased by 0.2 8 per cent and 2.3 4 per cent respectively, and the minor party vote fell to 1 4.7 1 per cent.

Amanda asserts, in a different context, that "progressive [i.e. people like us] voters in both major parties defected to the Greens". She seems to believe that she knows not just net gains and losses but the intermediate changes that make up the totals. Nobody knows, or can know, what these intermediate changes are.

The combined Democrats/Greens vote peaked in 1 9 9 0 at 1 2.5 9 per cent. It has not subsequently been above 1 0.3 7 per cent. The record-low 1 9 9 8 major party vote was a function of One Nation's meteoric rise, not of a swing to the Greens and the Democrats.

The number of Greens candidates increased steadily from 5 3 in 1 9 9 0 to 1 5 0 in 2 0 0 1. Some of the higher vote should be attributed to that, not to an increase in "core support".

It is also possible (probable?) that most of the 2 0 0 1 increase in the Greens vote came from One Nation defectors. In July 1 9 9 8, an IPA *Backgrounder* by WA Chamber of Commerce and Industry Director Lynden Rowe was published. In it, Rowe quoted from their own websites the three minor parties' policies. The responses were almost identical. All three identified themselves – and still do – as economic xenophobes opposed to international trade and free markets and in favour of highly regulated labour markets and financial institutions. All are for zero net immigration or something very close to it. Conversely, the Greens and Democrats are also in favour of an open-door entry policy for "refugees" or, more accurately, anyone who claims to be a refugee.

The Senate

The Senate election table (page 6 0, QE8) cannot be fully reconciled with the Parliamentary Handbook. It shows from 1 9 9 6 a Greens vote of 1.6 6 per cent and a WA Greens vote of 0.5 2 per cent, a total of 2.1 8 per cent. The

Handbook shows the Australian Greens vote to be 2.40 per cent, WA Greens 0.52 per cent and Tasmanian Greens 0.25 per cent, a total of 3.15 per cent – higher, in fact, than the total Green vote in 1998.

The 3.13 per cent decline in the 1998 vote for the major parties had nothing to do with "defections" to the Greens or the Democrats, both of which went down, but to the emergence of One Nation with 8.99 per cent of the vote.

State elections

Greens boosterism characterises Lohrey's coverage of state elections in Western Australia and Tasmania. Lohrey acknowledges the importance of One Nation's quirky decision in Western Australia to allocate preferences against sitting members and therefore to Labor's advantage, but fails to mention the long-festering Finance Broker's scandal and Richard Court's stupid refusal to remove promptly the relevant minister, Alfred Cove MLA Doug Shave, from the Cabinet or even to another ministry. Shave lost his own safe seat because Labor decided not to run a candidate. The Liberals repaid that opportunism in the 2002 Cunningham by-election.

The Greens, as they usually do, withheld preference decisions to give them more time to extort policy concessions and make a better judgement about who would win. Very late in the campaign, after the Liberals had shot themselves in both feet, the Greens backed Labor. It had no more effect on the election outcome than One Nation's de facto support for Labor, because neither party's preferences was effectively delivered.

In the Legislative Council, five Greens were, as Lohrey says, elected on 3 or 4 per cent of the primary vote or less. One of them was elected only because some One Nation votes were counted twice. The three Greens who got 4 per cent or less of the primary vote would not have been elected without the iniquitous "tick a box" system under which preferences are allocated. They polled 7 per cent and got five seats. One Nation polled 9 per cent and got three.

Last year's Tasmanian election is claimed to be a "Greens' triumph", apparently because the Greens won four seats after the Liberal vote collapsed. Lohrey attributes the higher Greens vote to the "widespread disgust at the (Labor) government's aggressive take it or leave it forestry policy". So "widespread" was this "disgust" that Labor won 52 per cent of the primary vote and 14 of the 25 seats. The Liberals, after playing footsies with Greens about an anti-Labor, anti-timber industry deal, won seven seats.

If that is a "Greens' triumph", may there be many more.

It is true that on present trends the Greens will be the most important minor party, due principally to the Democrats' self-destruction. But trends do change.

In the early 1 9 9 0s there were two Greens Senators from WA. They have now been defeated by Democrats. Present Greens triumphalism may yet be illusory.

In three of the four federal elections in the 1 9 6 0s, the Democratic Labor Party had a higher primary vote than the Greens have yet recorded. And unlike the Greens, DLP preferences were highly disciplined and always directed against Labor. In two, possibly three of the 1 9 6 0s elections, DLP preferences were decisive to the result. The DLP has had no relevance to any federal election outcome since 1 9 6 9.

The Greens' quality assessment

On page 1 2, Amanda states, "The environment movement never was anti-rational and science was and remains one of the most potent weapons in the green movement's arsenal of polemics."

That (pseudo) science is a major component of "the green movement's arsenal of polemics" is true. But real science plays little, if any, part in their policy determination. A few examples:

The precautionary principle. A central component of green ideology which asserts that no new technology can be adopted unless it has been proved there will be no adverse side effects. This entails proving a negative, which, I understand, is regarded as logically impossible. Greens want the "precautionary" principle to replace rational assessment of risk – a Renaissance concept later developed by scientists and statisticians – as the probability theory which determines the modern view of the world and public policy.

The absurdity of the precautionary principle can be demonstrated by its retrospective application to immunology, which often does have undesirable side effects. Ipso facto, it should be banned leaving millions of people to die in the "natural" way. For a comprehensive review of this matter see Peter Bernstein's *Against the Gods*.

Prohibition of all offshore oil exploration. The annual stormwater run-off from urban areas puts more petroleum into the sea than nearly fifty years of offshore exploration and production. Petroleum is readily biodegradable in a marine environment.

The green mantra that modern agriculture is "unsustainable" and must be replaced by organic agriculture. Never mind that modern agriculture is immensely productive, feeding an ever-increasing population much better than in any previous era and at massively lower, and still declining, real costs. It is no coincidence that organic farming is the norm in the same places where endemic malnutrition and sporadic mass starvation is the norm. Greens, or most of them at least, are not deranged despots like Robert Mugabe who prefers to let his people starve in order to protect them from the alleged health hazard of GM food, but if their organic farming fantasy is enforced, millions more will die of starvation.

Forest management and timber harvesting. "Preservation of old growth forests" is cited by Lohrey as an important objective of the Greens. It is also one of the most irrational. The language reveals the mindset. No forest can be "preserved". One century's "old growth" forest is the next century's dead forest.

The science and management of forests has long been a minimum four-year degree course at Melbourne University and ANU. When forest policy was being made in Western Australia, professional foresters were sidelined and ignored. Policy was determined by a motley collection including a football coach, a dress designer, an Archbishop, a doctor of medicine, a one-time hurdler and a nonagenarian nonentity. Their common attributes were self-indulgence, giant-size egos and a profound ignorance of forest science and management. Politicians – on both sides, though Labor was worse – succumbed to their demands and locked away enough forest to put another thousand vulnerable blue-collar workers out of jobs and devastate timber communities. The Greens, of course, were most strident supporters of that policy. So much for Amanda's claim that the Greens are custodians of compassion and social justice.

What about the forests?

One kilometre east of the small one-time timber township of Northcliffe (twenty-nine kilometres south of Pemberton) is a picnic reserve called Forest Park and a walking track called Marri Meander. The park is home to a mixed karri/marri forest with a dense understorey and trees so old they are falling down in large numbers. This is a preview of the future for all of the sacred "old growth forest". No seedlings are emerging and none will until the forest is burned. Its accumulated fuel load is big enough to ensure every living plant will be killed when, not if, a wildfire razes it. The forest will then regenerate.

What drives deep greens?

Consciously or not, Amanda confirms that green ideology is a secular religious movement. Thus, "This is the Greens' own Genesis story and Pedder is its paradise lost," and "the [Pedder] campaign was fought with a quasi-mystical fervour," and "The growth of this international ecology movement has been accompanied by the rise in an earth-based spirituality."

Similar mystical sentiments can be found in B.A. Santamaria's writing. Anna Branwell's *Ecology in the Twentieth Century: A History* (1 9 8 9) points to the role of such sentiments in Nazi ideology. Greens are not Nazis, but their secular religion, like that of the medieval Church and modern Christian and Islamic fundamentalism, has a mystical, intolerant and authoritarian streak.

Not surprisingly, Bob Brown is seen to be this secular religion's Messiah. He is fulsomely praised for increasing the Greens' electoral appeal to peaceniks by jumping on the anti-Iraq war bandwagon. Surely Amanda, herself a Tasmanian, knows about Brown's speech to the Tasmanian Parliament on 4 April 1 9 9 1. Brown moved the motion:

> The House calls on the Prime Minister, Bob Hawke, to act immediately to intervene in Iraq to stop the slaughter of the Kurds and establish their right to self-determination ... we are in the disgusting position of sitting on our hands while these people are absolutely slaughtered – the least we can do is get our Prime Minister to speak up and put the full weight of this country towards the protection of these innocents.

Why hasn't Brown been confronted with this bit of his own history in any of his frequent TV interviews and doorstops? Is he a protected species?

The moral humbug exhibited by Brown on this issue is consistent with his party's failure to support Peter Costello's attempt, in the face of a dishonest motor lobby campaign, to maintain petrol excise indexation.

For all of human history until the last two centuries, the vast majority of people knew nothing better than subsistence as a living standard. Most people were employed in the – not always successful – attempt to produce enough food to sustain life. Life was indeed mostly "poor, nasty, brutish and short".

In modern times, almost everyone in the first world has a standard of living beyond the conceptual grasp, let alone the experience, of the ruling class of great empires.

It began, necessarily, with the agricultural revolution which started about 2 0 0 years ago and has not stopped. This revolution vastly increased output and labour productivity, freeing labour for new industries. A vastly greater population is now much better fed at a continually falling real cost.

Other factors aiding the transition from scarcity to abundance are:

—Scientific, technical and mechanical innovation;

—Capital accumulation;

—Market economies and international trade; and

—Cheap abundant energy from fossil fuels.

The Greens are opposed to all of them. They are strident and scary supporters of self-serving Kyoto Protocol scenarios.

The CO_2-induced global warming hypothesis has been discredited by twenty-five years of satellite-measured global temperature. The economic component of IPCC models has been demolished by former Australian Statistician Ian Castles. He has received no reply. I doubt that he ever will. Even if there was a problem, Graham Pearman, head of the CSIRO Division of Atmospheric Physics and a global warming advocate, has admitted Kyoto would make "hardly any difference".

A relatively small amount of cheaper non-fossil fuel energy could be produced from hydro power. Vast quantities could be produced at somewhat higher cost from nuclear reactors. Predictably, the Greens veto both.

The Greens agenda poses a threat to affluence and, because of the consequences of large reductions in real incomes, a threat to political harmony. Some of them know this very well: it is their objective.

Who are the deep greens?

A substantial proportion come from remnants of defunct communist parties. A younger group would probably be communists if the parties were viable. Their objective is to destroy the capitalist system with economic sabotage.

Some are driven by power lust and the opportunity to exercise political power without accountability. A lot of mostly younger people just want to thumb their nose at society and its institutions. A large number are probably genuinely concerned about clean air, water and physical beauty – who isn't? – but are victims of green exaggeration.

The organic agriculture lobby and the suppliers of high-cost solar and wind energy are eager to acquire, via political fiat, captive markets for their non-competitive products – like Renewable Energy Bills. Plus of course there are the rent seekers in academia whose incomes and status are dependent on the greenhouse "industry".

Peter Walsh

Amanda Lohrey

I'll start with the trees and move on to the wood.

—Peter Walsh disputes the figures on the vote for the major parties in recent elections but the difference in question is just over 1 per cent. In terms of trends over a long period this is not a significant variation.[1] The political point lies in overall trends over time – and several elections – and the trend to the Greens has been acknowledged by senior political analysts within both major parties and across the media.

—Every election adversarial commentators talk down Greens gains. Every gain is a local or temporary effect, some kind of fluke or anomaly which the numbers men of the Labor Party are at pains to explain away in the minutiae. To ascribe Court's demise in Western Australia to his failure to sack Shave from cabinet and to rate this above an outpouring of public angst about forests – so passionate it led to an unprecedented breakaway group from the WA Liberal Party – is as good an instance of myopic rationalisation as you could hope to find.

—The triumph of the Greens in Tasmania stands. It lies not in their preventing a Labor victory but in making an electoral comeback after both major parties had combined to alter the entire Hare-Clark electoral system in order to purge them from the Tasmanian lower house. Currently the Tasmanian Liberals show no signs of revival and the Greens are regarded as the de facto opposition. This may well be phase one of bigger things for the Greens, but whether it is or not, not even Peter Walsh can gainsay the extent of their rebound from the threat of electoral annihilation.

—Walsh makes much of the evanescence of One Nation but the Greens have been around a lot longer and survived major assault and battery (see Tasmania). They have consolidated their party structures where those of One Nation have disintegrated and they have an experienced and credible second-and third-tier leadership. Finally, they are part of a growing international political alliance.

Bob Brown is consulted by cabinet ministers in European governments. If the same can be said for Pauline Hanson, she has yet to make this known.

—Early in his response Peter Walsh suggests that the rise of the minor party vote is much more to do with the fortunes of One Nation and that this invalidates my claims for the Greens. A few lines later he writes, "It is possible (probable?) that most of the 2001 increase in the Greens vote came from One Nation defectors" which would appear to contradict the earlier assertion, and he goes on to suggest that Greens and One Nation voters may be all of a kind, "economic xenophobes" who swing from one minor party to the other. This one-size-fits-all account of current disaffection relies for its source on no less than the IPA, the oldest right-wing propaganda organisation in Australia and one of those I refer to in my essay as having been credited by Alex Carey (*Taking the Risk out of Democracy*) with consistently promoting a corporate agenda in public life. One wonders where Walsh would place those apparently anomalous free traders like John Hewson who now so forcefully speak up for the ratification of the Kyoto Agreement, and who are one of the manifestations of that change in sensibility, across the spectrum, that my essay sets out to document.

—The rhetorical elision that brackets the late B. A. Santamaria alongside the Nazis is unforgivable. Both are lumped into the same broad band because their political philosophies had "quasi-mystical" underpinnings. On that basis we should ban all religious and spiritual movements and be done with it. This is techno-reason gone mad.

—Walsh accuses Bob Brown of hypocrisy and opportunism for trying to "increase the Greens' electoral appeal" by "jumping on the anti-Iraq war bandwagon". In fact, Brown began his political activism not as an environmental but as a peace activist against visiting US nuclear submarines (p. 75, *Groundswell*). Did Walsh read *all* of my essay or only bits? Brown's call for intervention on behalf of the Kurds belongs in the category of the UN intervention in the former Yugoslavia or East Timor and only the ultra-tendentious could begin to equate it with the recent US invasion of Iraq.

—Isn't it a bit late for a revival of the reds-under-the-bed scare? To argue that a substantial proportion of Greens "come from remnants of defunct communist parties" shows just how little first-hand knowledge Walsh has of the green movement or of the younger generation. I first realised that I was middle-aged when I conducted a seminar which included some of the best and brightest students at a leading Australian university in the mid-1990s and discovered that not one of the students present knew what the Cuban missile crisis had been. Two of them knew who Fidel Castro was and only one of them had ever heard of Trotsky.

—Peter Walsh can take up his objections to Greens' policies with the members and supporters of the Greens Party. The project of my essay was to document a shift in Australian political sensibility and its reflection in changes to our political landscape over the past thirty years. It was not my project to critique current policy debates within the Greens, or indeed the environment movement at large. There are passionate debates within both on a number of issues and there are significant disagreements, just as there are in any political party, and in all these debates community consultation is vital. Walsh's objection to community input to WA forestry policy by "a motley collection including a football coach, a dress designer, an Archbishop, a doctor of medicine, a one-time hurdler and a nonagenarian nonentity" would seem to indicate a contempt for the democratic process and a worrying reliance on entrenched administrations that fall back on arguments of "expertise" to disguise their own value positions. Since when has any form of expertise ever been value-free? The expertise in Forestry Tasmania has long been under a cloud. Not only that, when my husband was the Tasmanian Minister for Forests (for a very short time until the anti-green lobby persuaded the then premier that he was a threat) he was regularly bailed up during his electoral rounds by forestry workers at the grass roots who were most unhappy with the official line taken by their senior management and the way in which on-the-ground data was being misinterpreted or ignored. Whose "expertise" was at stake there? (Among anti-woodchipping lobby groups to emerge in Tasmania you'll find Timber Workers for Forests.)

Oh, and by the way, could that "nonagenarian nonentity" from WA that Walsh refers to have been Dame Rachel Cleland, a founding member of the WA Liberal Party?

Peter Walsh's response to *Groundswell* is a snapshot of the reasons why so many people are disenchanted with the Australian Labor Party. When Peter Walsh was in government he headed up the various razor gangs that were so bent on surgically pruning and removing the trees that they failed to take account of the overall health of the wood. In the course of my research for *Groundswell* I repeatedly came into contact with former members of the ALP who were angry and bitter in their critique of the Labor Party, and the former Minister for Finance was not spoken of fondly. I omitted most of this material because it was not my purpose to write an exercise in Labor bashing but to examine the ways in which the Greens had come into being as a political force in their own right, and not just as a reaction to changes within the ALP (although these clearly were a factor).

The comment often made to me, particularly by former ALP members over forty, was that the ALP had once stood for a comprehensive vision of community and the commonwealth. Even at the height of Cold War divisions between the Left and Right wings of the party, common ground on social justice remained a vital moral substratum of the party such that in areas of social policy figures like B. A. Santamaria and Brian Harradine had more in common with the old Left than with the Walsh-style economic rationalists of contemporary Labor's putative "centre". There was a heart in the ALP, a light on the hill if you like, and it spoke to community and brotherhood. Some of this was Catholic welfarism and some the secularised Christian ethic of democratic socialism but both sides believed that they were their brother's keeper.

The environmental movement has extended that ethic to argue that we are the planet's keeper, the keepers of sustainable life. Within that broad position, the debates are fierce, not least on population control (as Tim Flannery's recent QE demonstrates) but there is a moral passion there that has been steadily leaching out of the ALP and its dispirited branches – now no more than backyard hatcheries for the factions. The old ALP was full of "believers", a category that Peter Walsh appears to sneer at, though he clearly is a believer of sorts himself (in the cargo cult of free trade). The old ALP was proud of its believers and when Keating triumphed in 1 9 9 3 I seem to recall the party issue of special t-shirts emblazoned with the words "True Believer". But where are the True Believers now? The answer to that is that many of them are voting Green. They have seen a gaggle of tin men in the guise of razor gangs remove the heart of the Labor Party and roast it over the coals of economic rationalism. All that is left is the cinders of the present Opposition, and a degraded public culture where an elite private school (Kings, Parramatta) can be given a government grant to build new polo stables while a swimming pool on a large public housing estate (Kensington, Melbourne) is filled in with sand.

Amanda Lohrey

1. All my figures were taken from the Australian Electoral Office and my charts were submitted to that office for verification.

A. Duncan Brown is Emeritus Professor of Biological Sciences at the University of Wollongong. He is the author of *Feed or Feedback: Agriculture, Population Dynamics and the State of the Planet* (International Books, Utrecht, in press).

Peter Christoff is Co-ordinator of Environmental Studies at the School of Anthropology, Geography and Environmental Studies (University of Melbourne). He is also a member of the Executive of the Australian Conservation Foundation and on the Board of Greenpeace Australia-Pacific.

Tim Flannery has made contributions of international significance to the fields of palaeontology, mammalogy and conservation. His books include *The Future Eaters*, *Throwim Way Leg* and *The Eternal Frontier*. He is the Director of the South Australian Museum.

Barney Foran is an environmental scientist and the co-author of the report for the federal government, *Future Dilemmas: Options to 2050 for Australia's Population, Technology, Resources and Environment*, which was published in November 2 0 0 2.

Gideon Haigh has written ten books on sport and business, including *The Battle for BHP* and *One of a Kind: The Story of Bankers Trust Australia 1969–1999*. He has won the Australian Cricket Society's Jack Pollard Trophy on four occasions, and his *Mystery Spinner: The Story of Jack Iverson* won England's PriceWaterhouseCoopers Prize for Cricket Book of the Year. He is a contributor to the *Bulletin* and has worked recently as a columnist for the *Guardian* and the *Times*.

Amanda Lohrey has published a number of articles and essays on Australian political life as well as two political novels, *The Morality of Gentlemen* and *The Reading Group*. Her most recent novel is the award-winning *Camille's Bread*.

George Seddon is Emeritus Professor of Environmental Science (University of Melbourne). Among his books are *Landprints* and *From the Country*, an anthology from the work of T.R. Garnett, which he edited.

Peter Walsh was Minister for Resources and Energy (1 9 8 3–8 4) and Minister for Finance (1 9 8 4–9 0) in the Hawke government. His memoirs, *Confessions of a Failed Finance Minister*, were published in 1 9 9 5. He is president of the Lavoisier Group.

QUARTERLY ESSAY

www.ingramcontent.com/pod-product-compliance
Lightning Source LLC
Chambersburg PA
CBHW041742290326
41931CB00052BA/3498